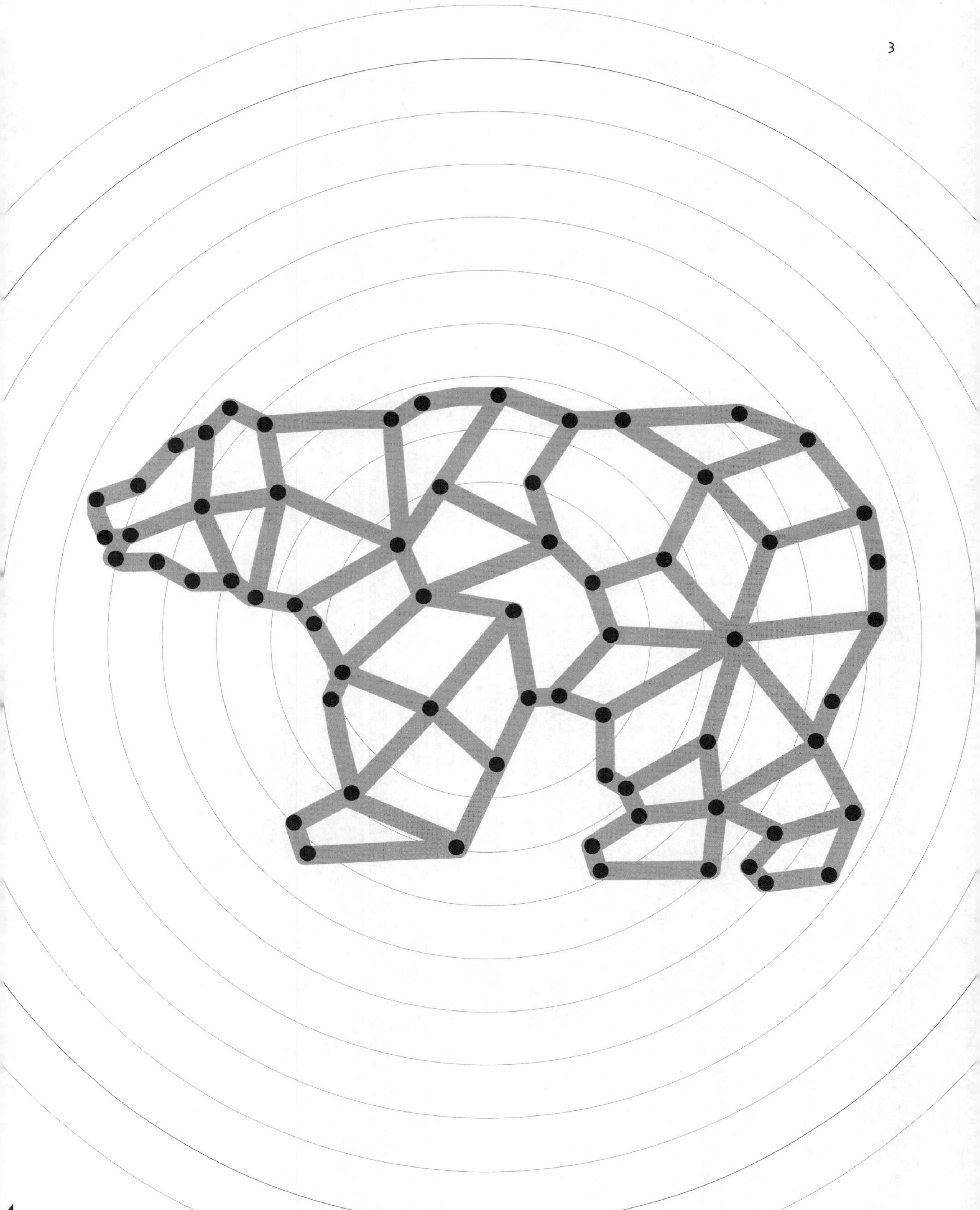

good luck

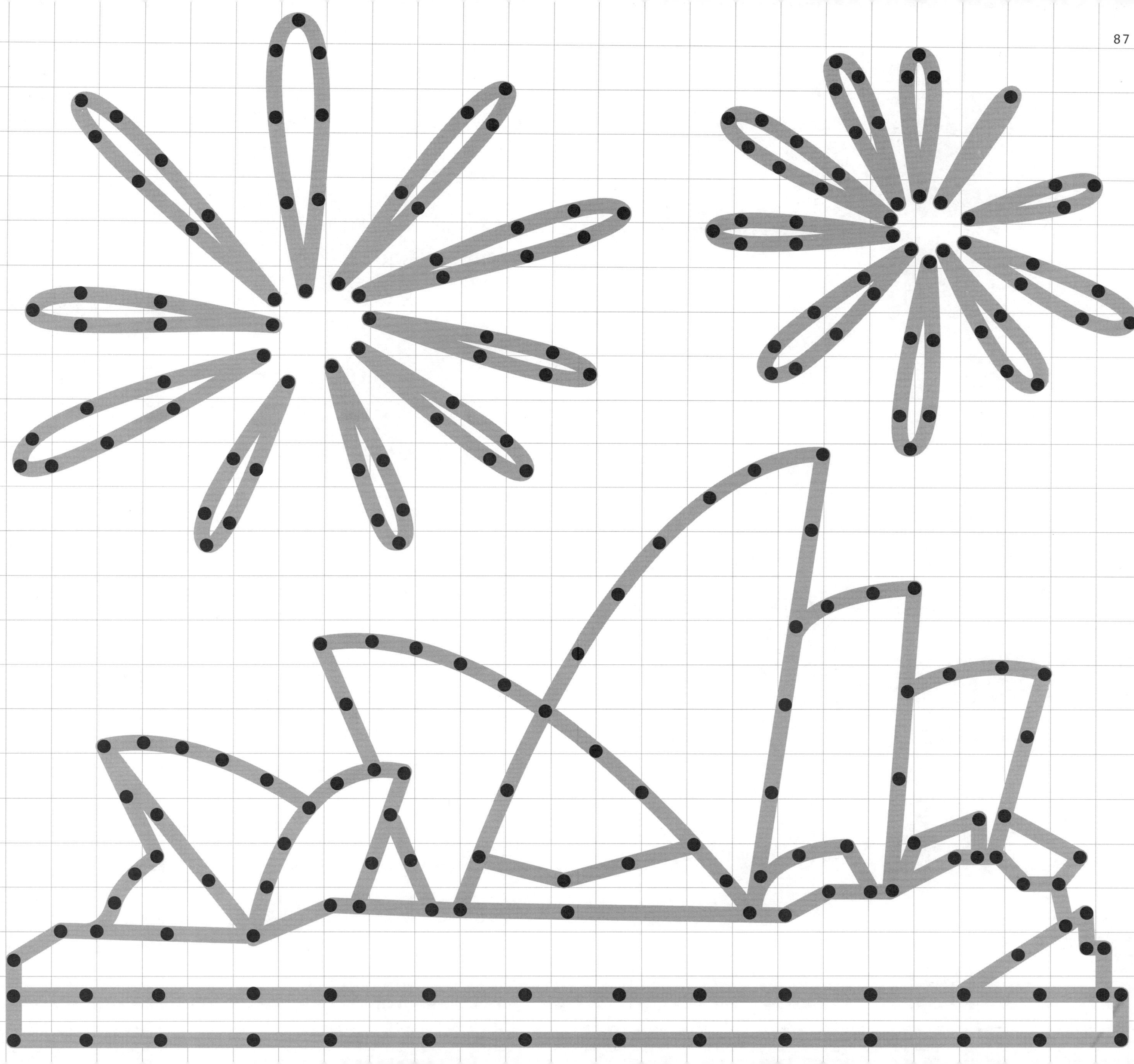

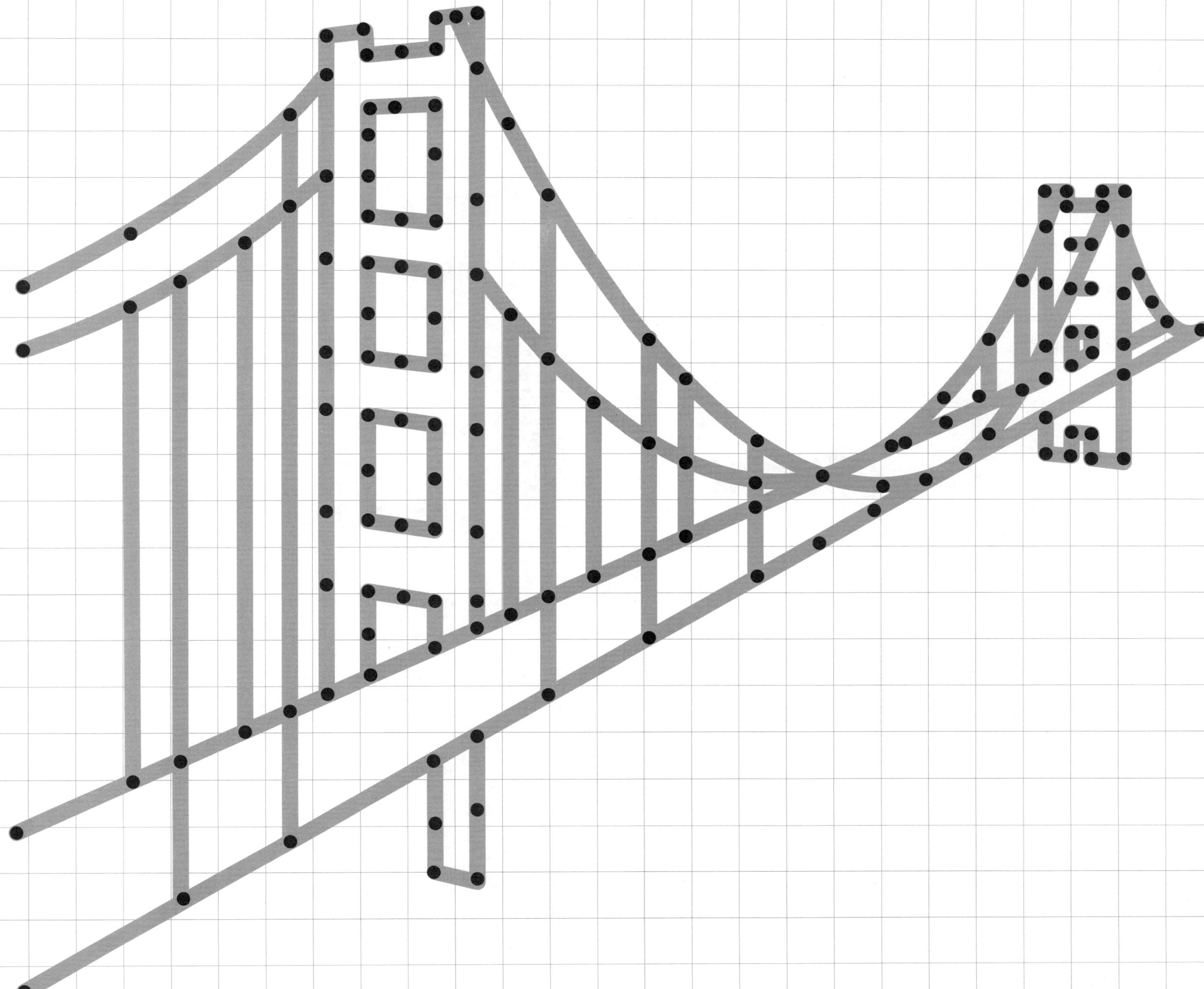

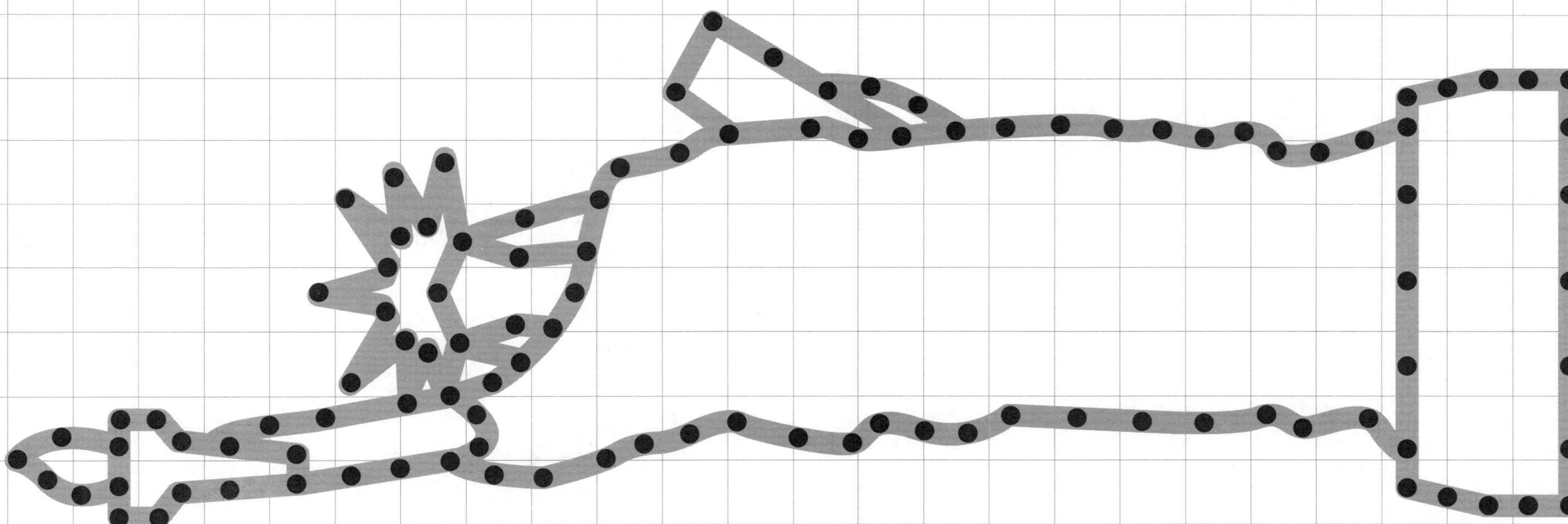

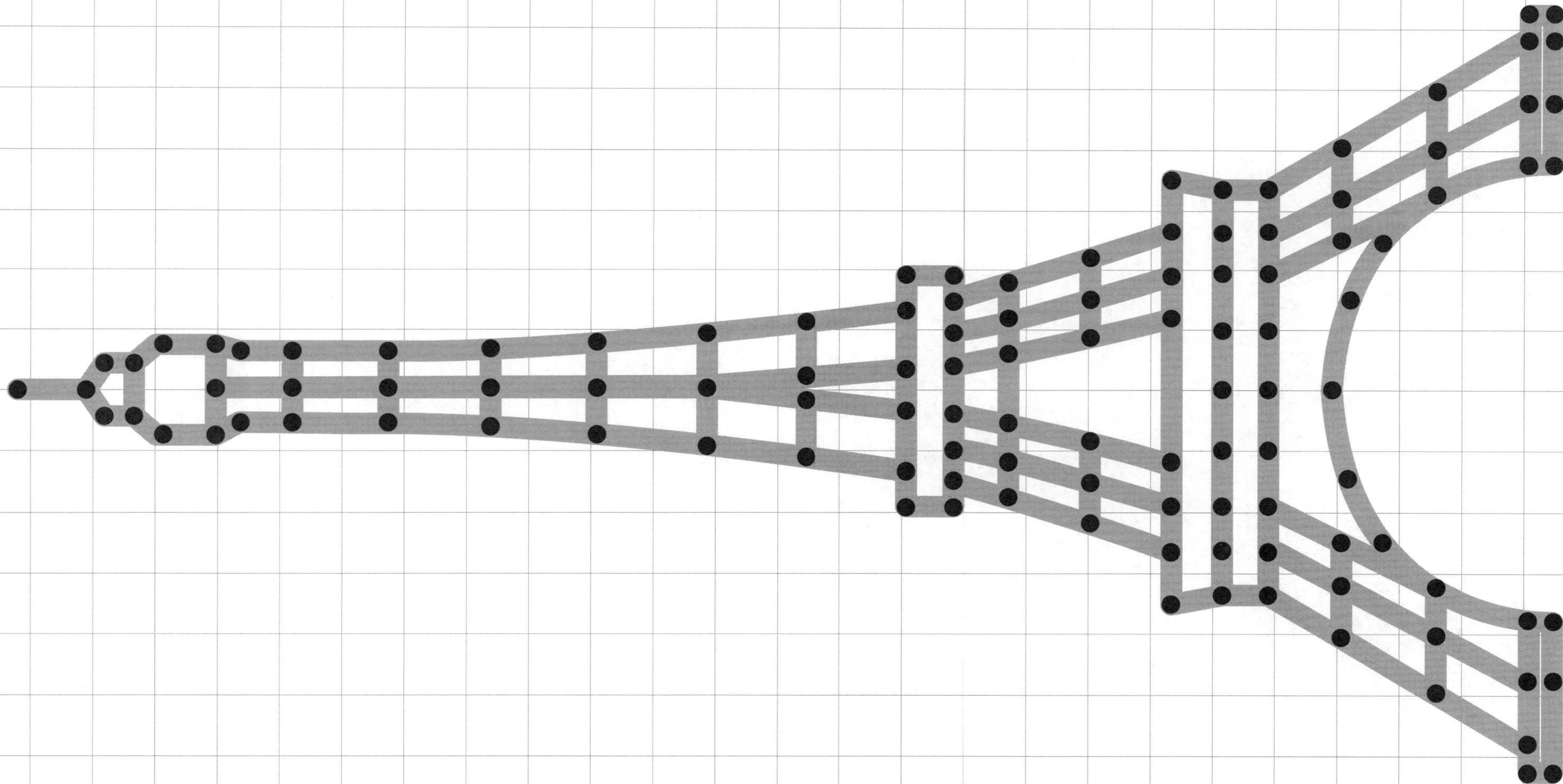

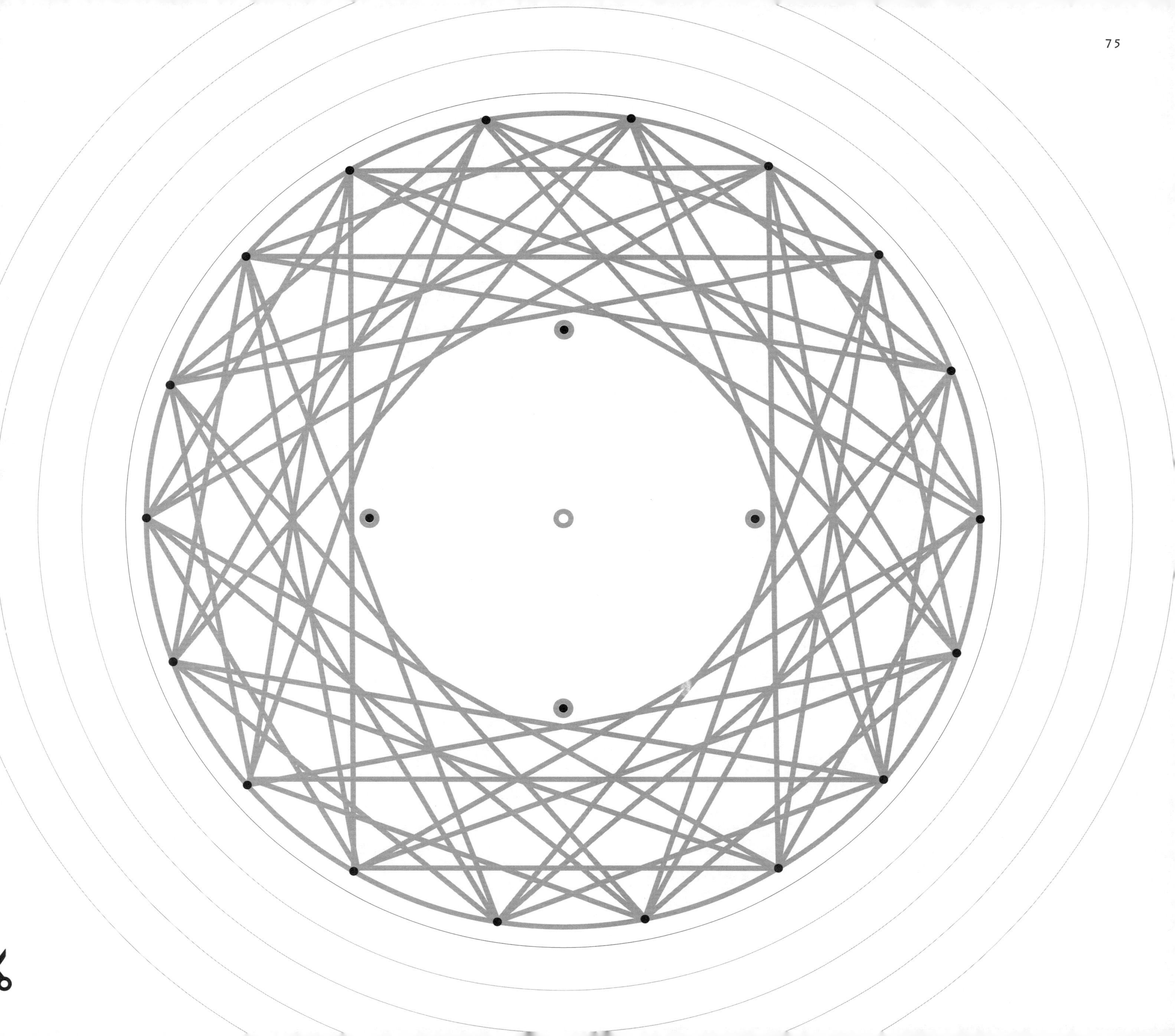

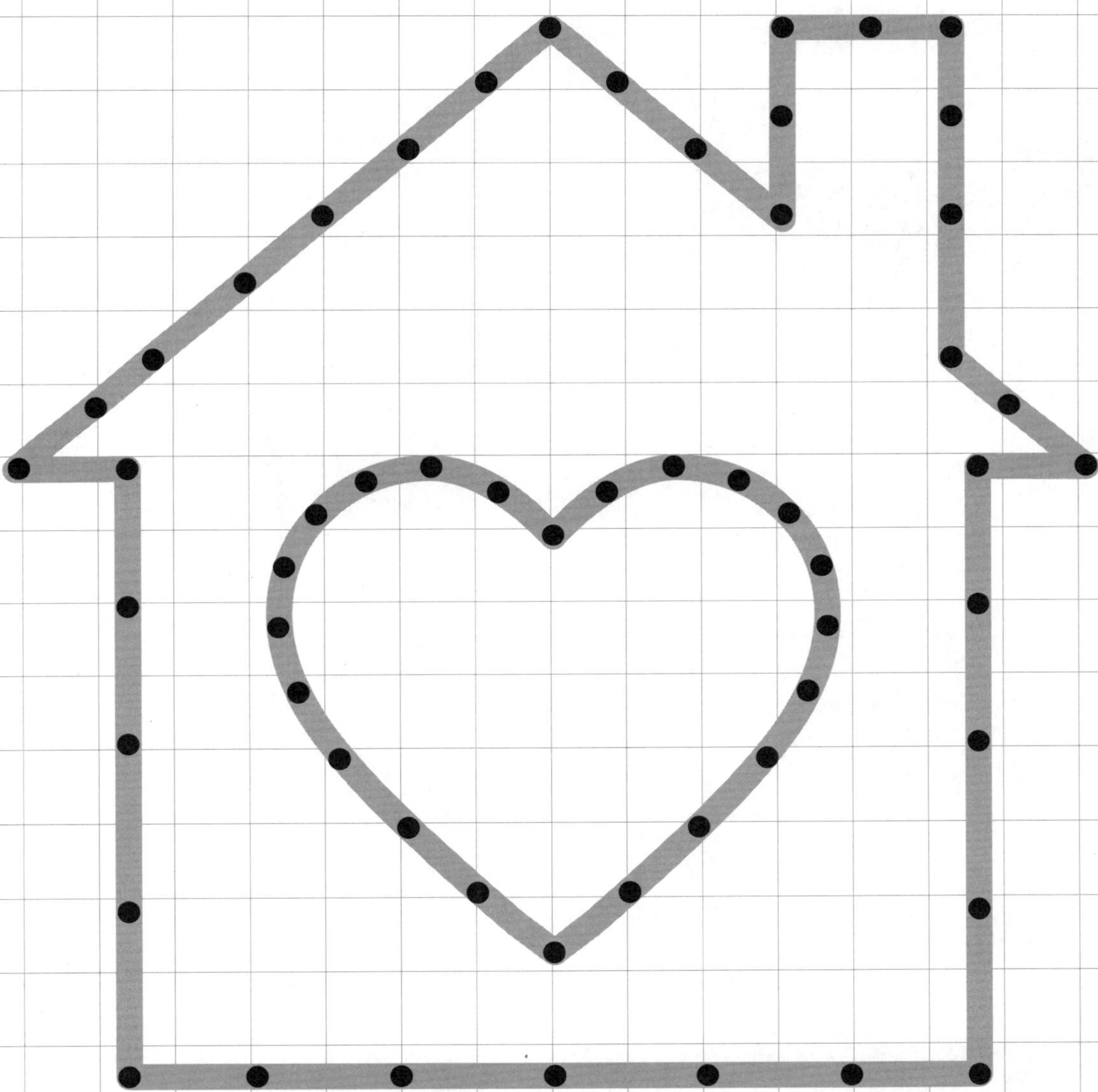

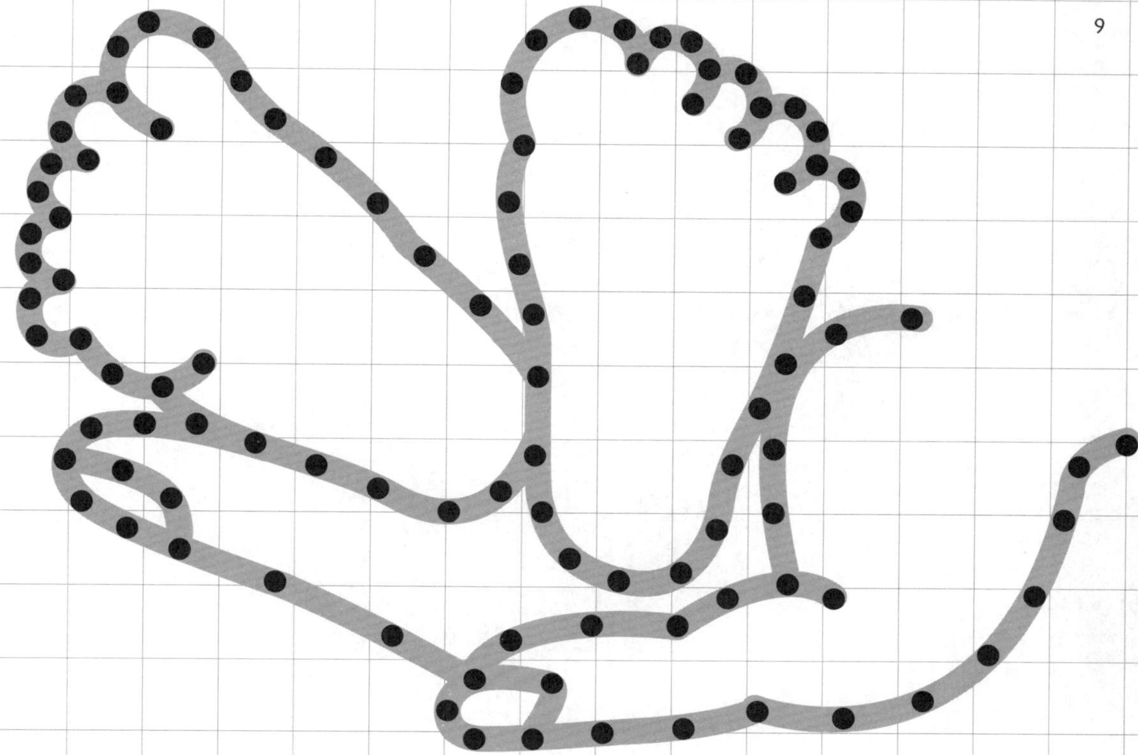

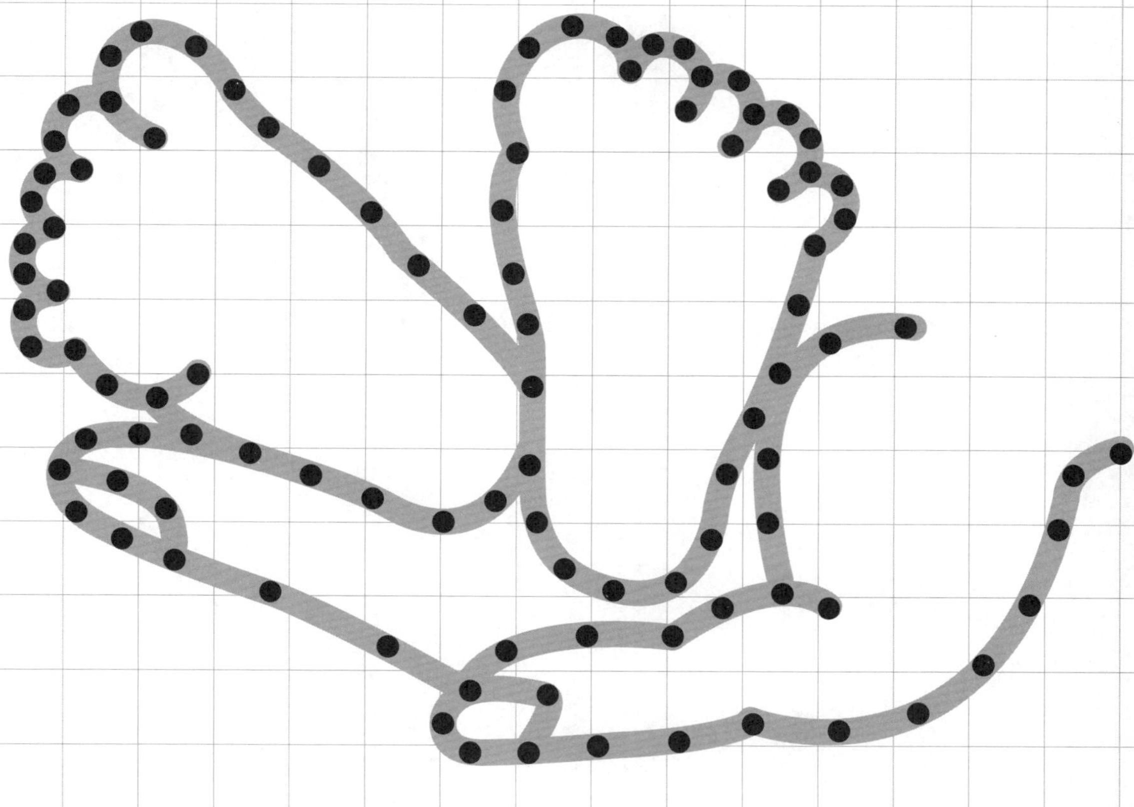

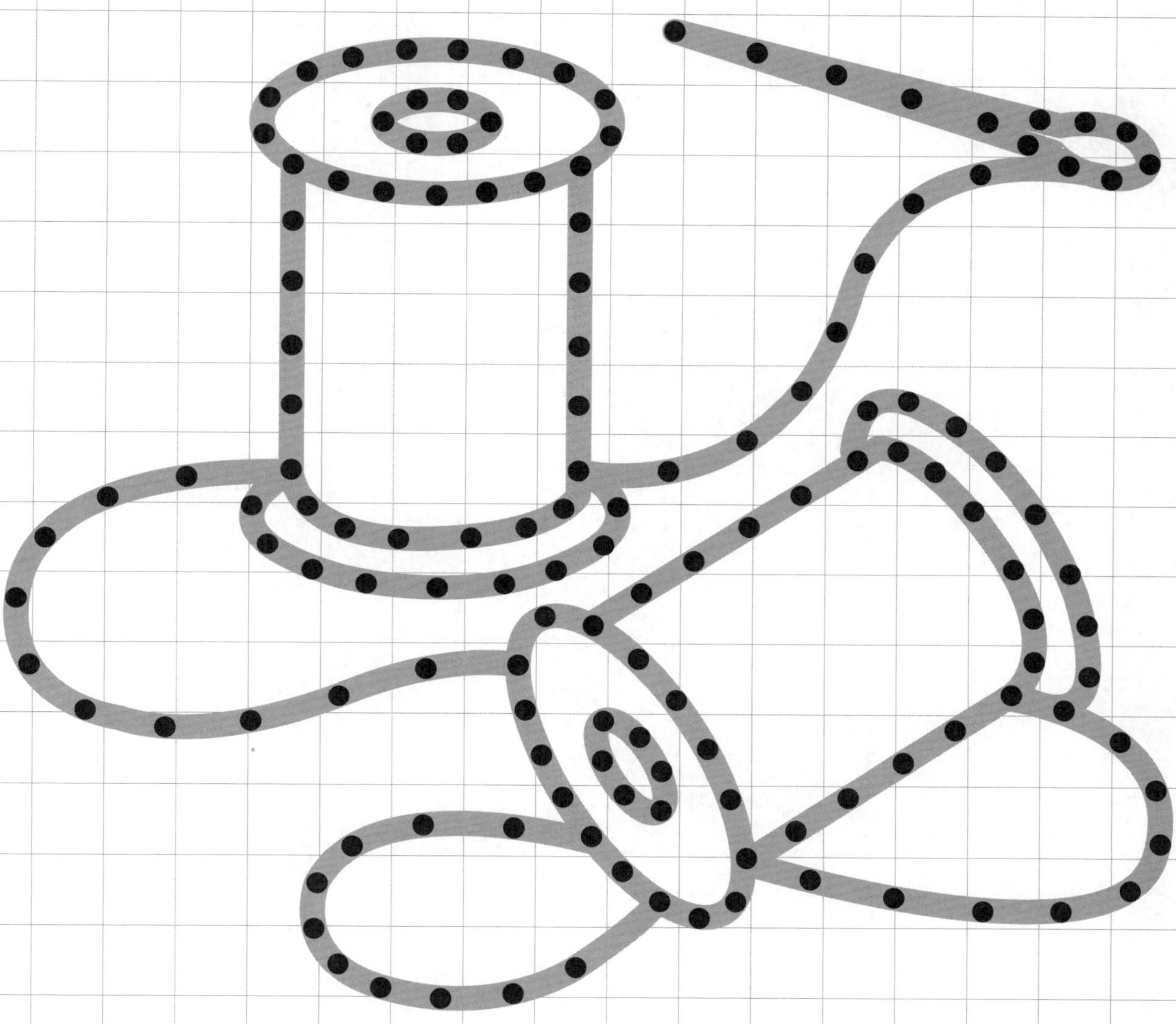

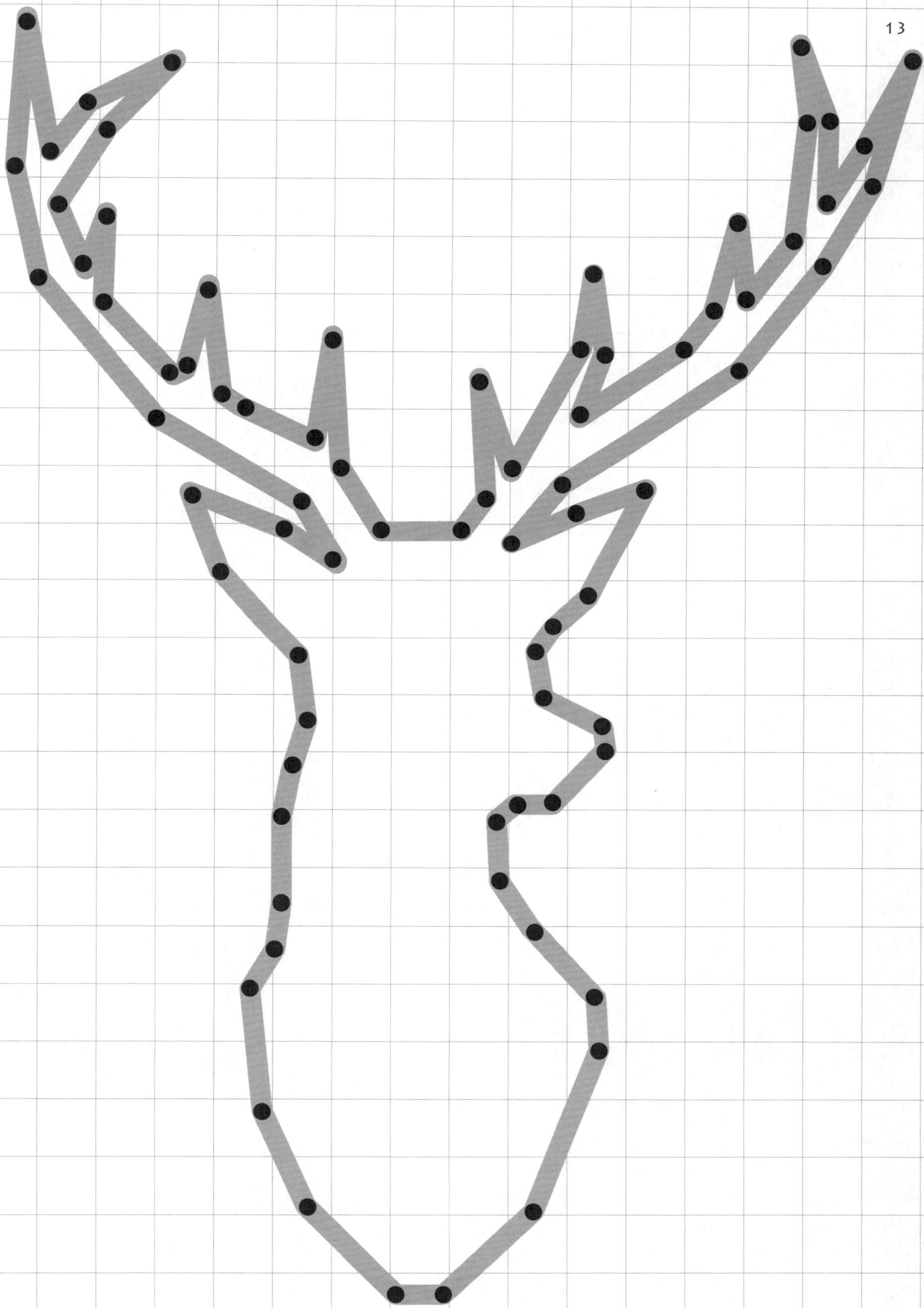

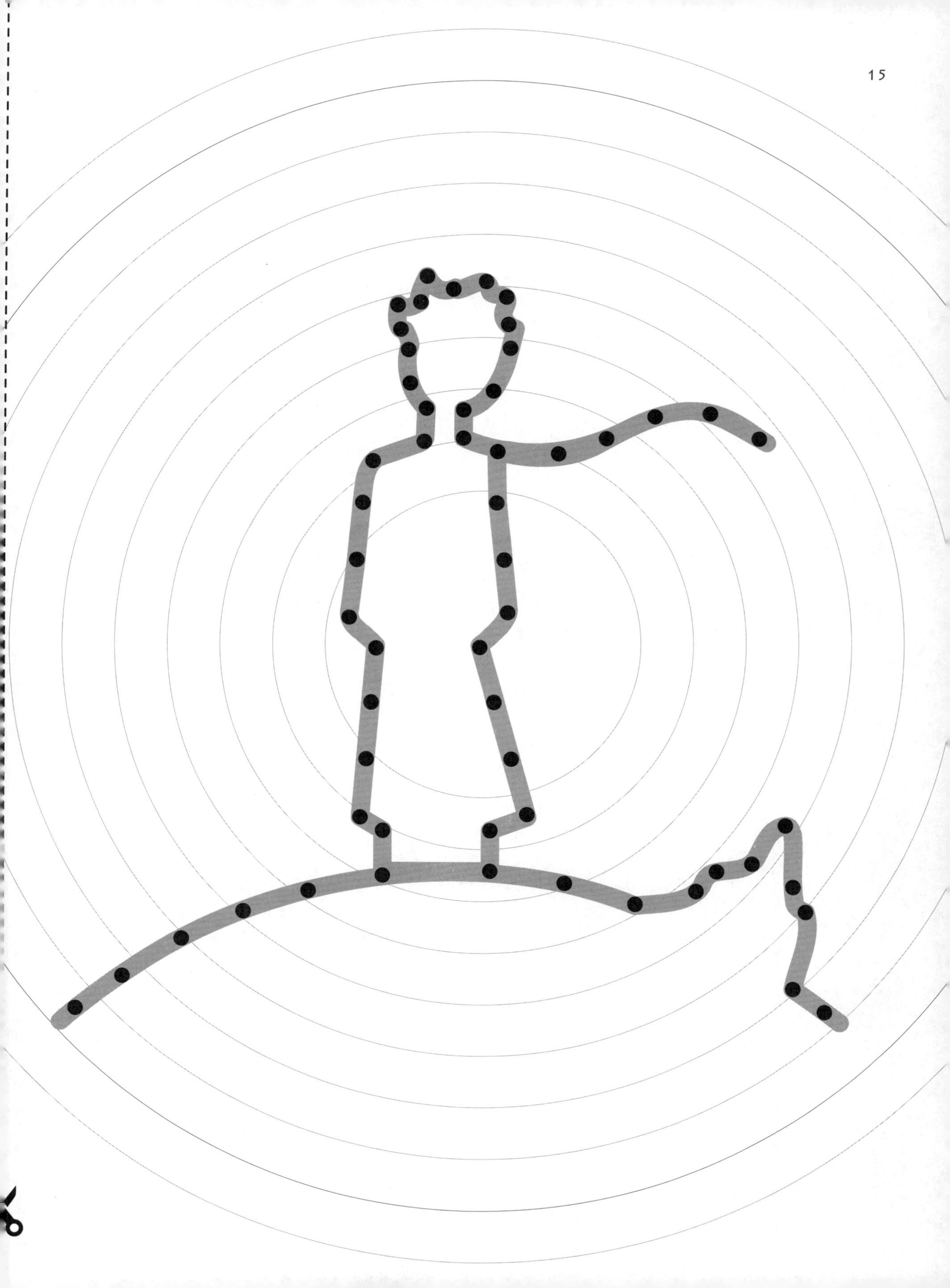

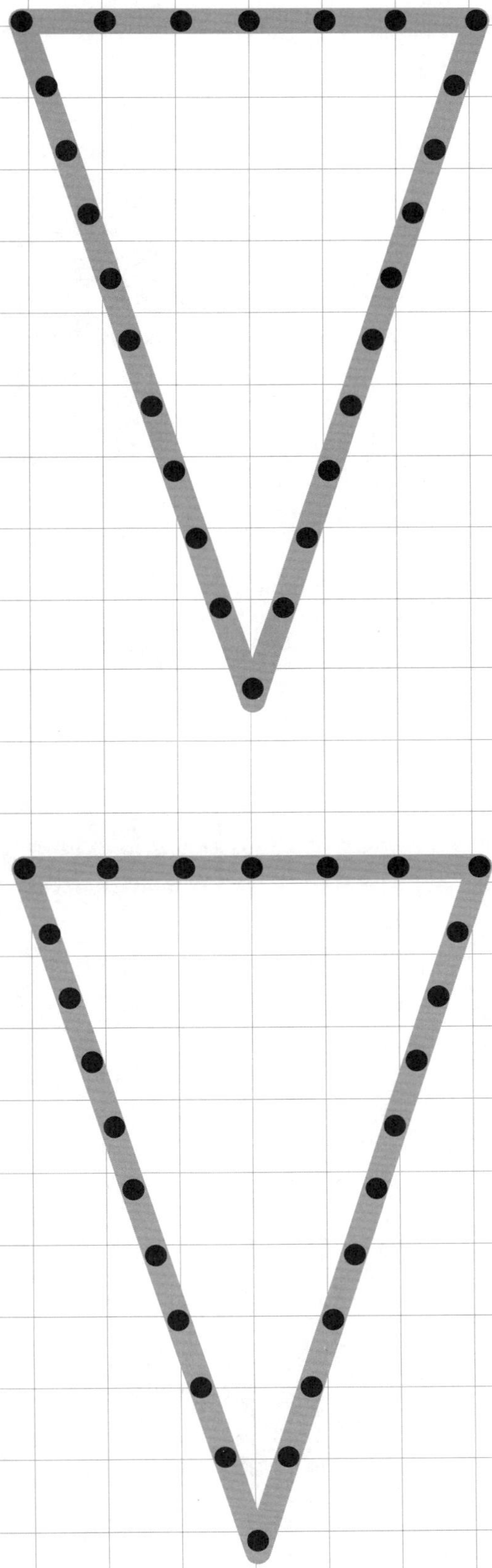

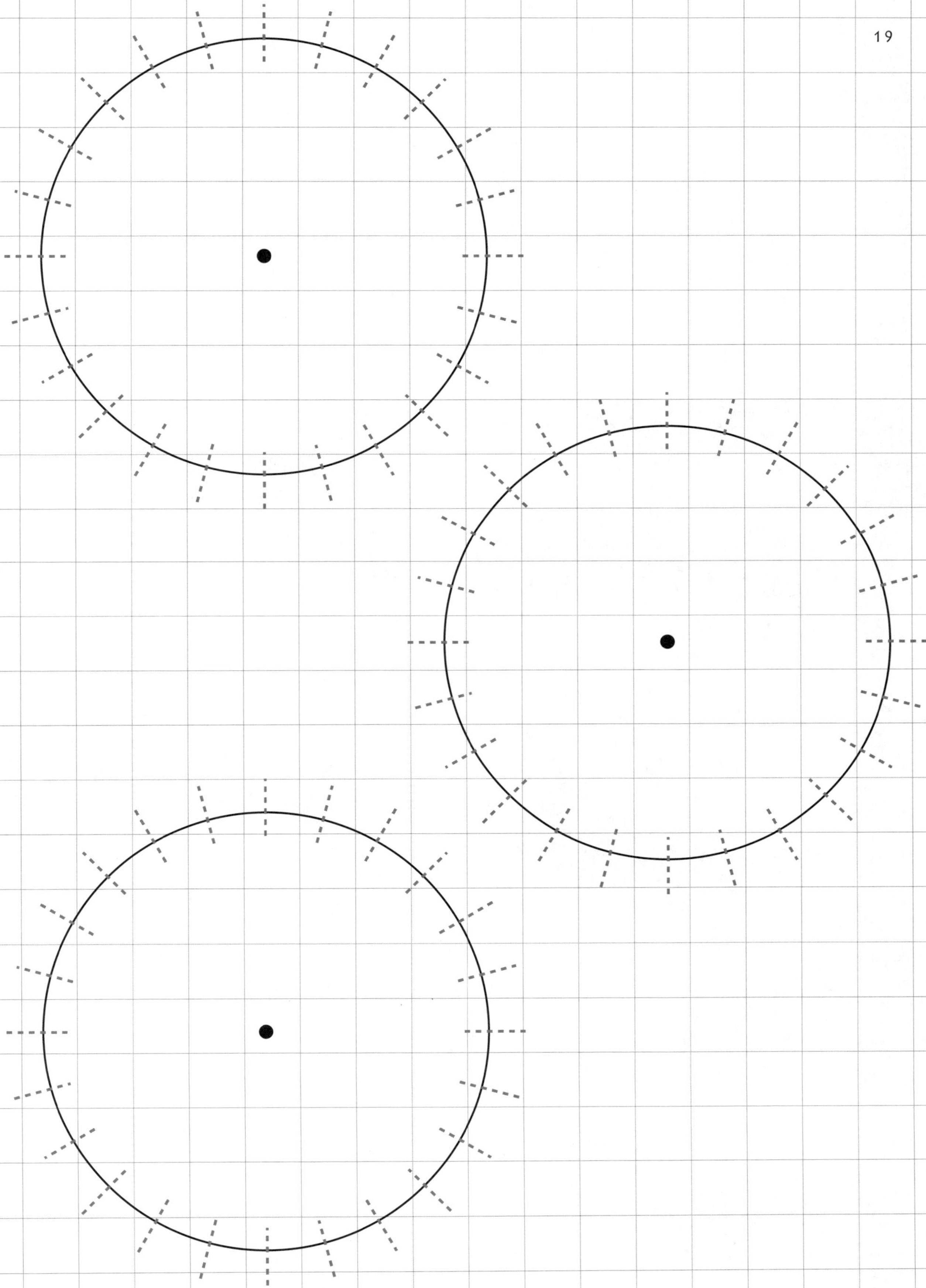

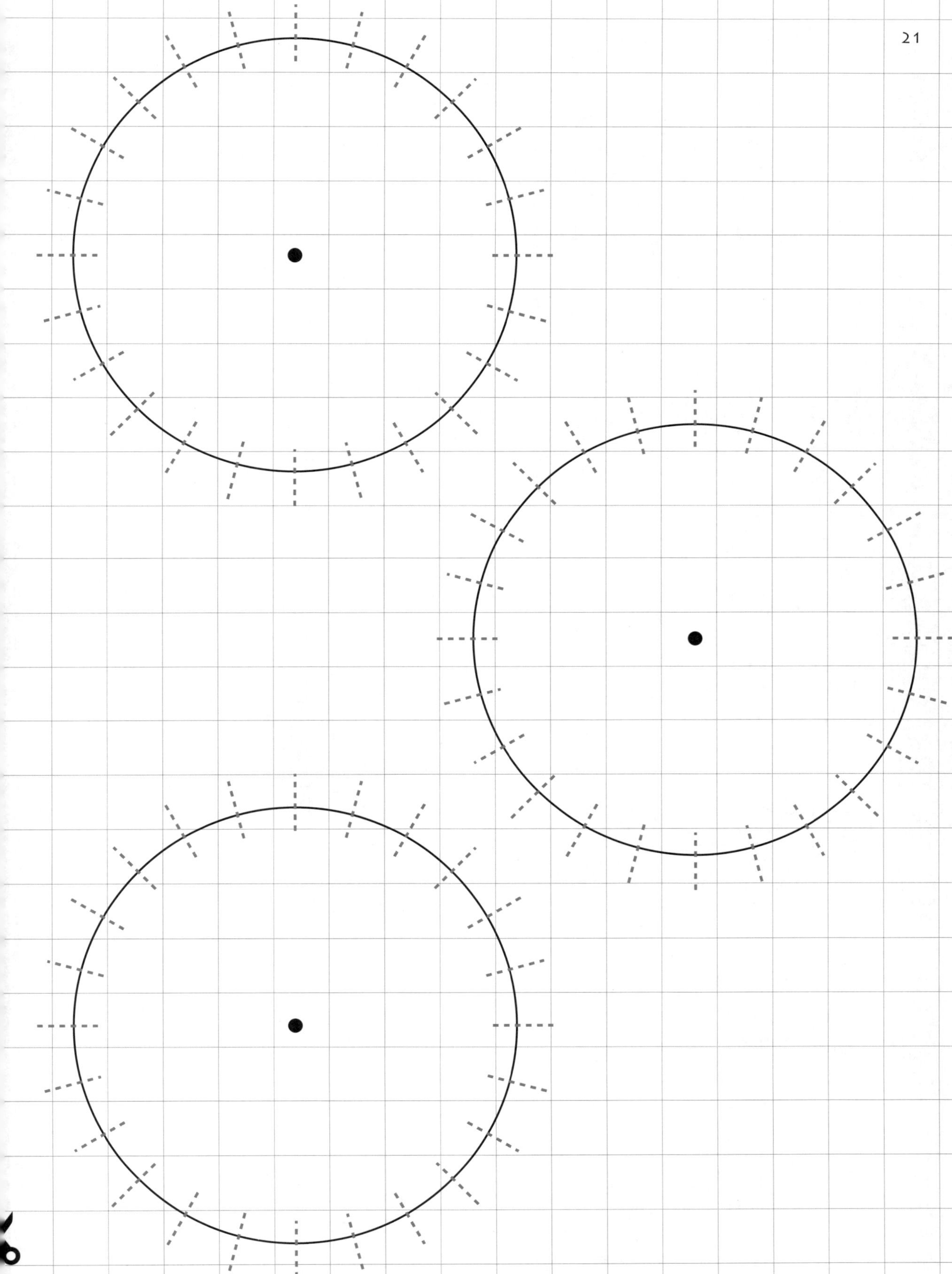

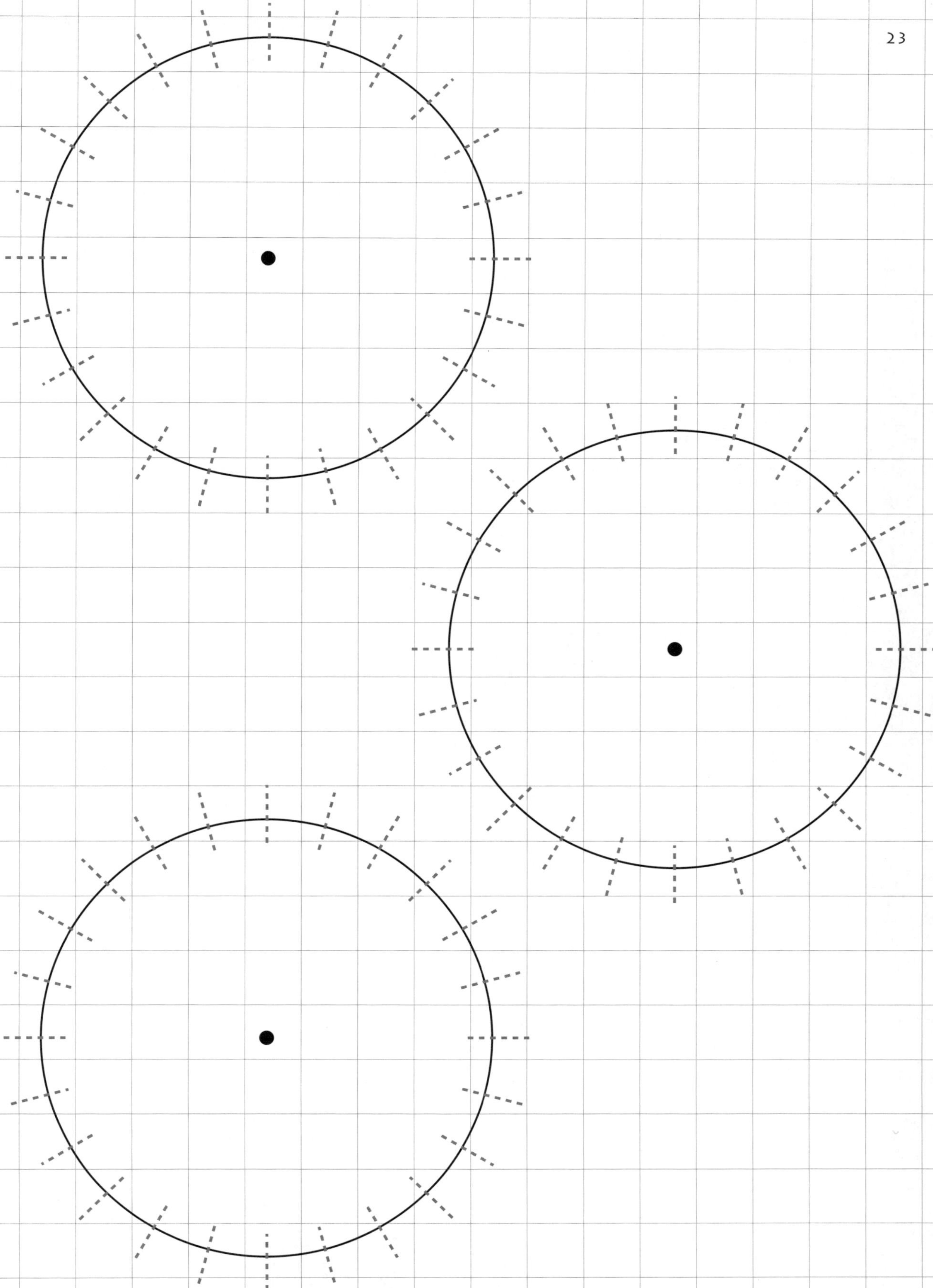

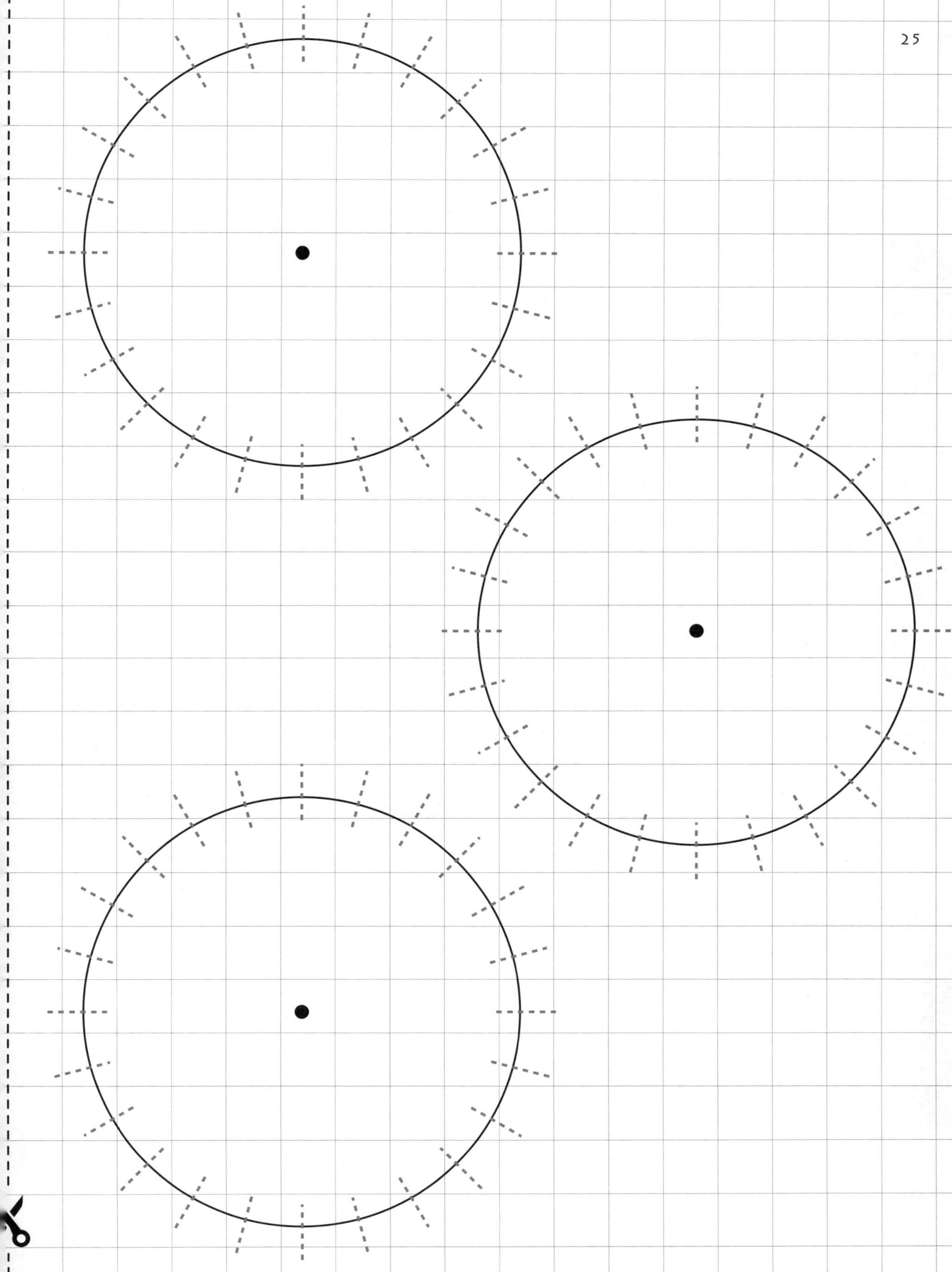

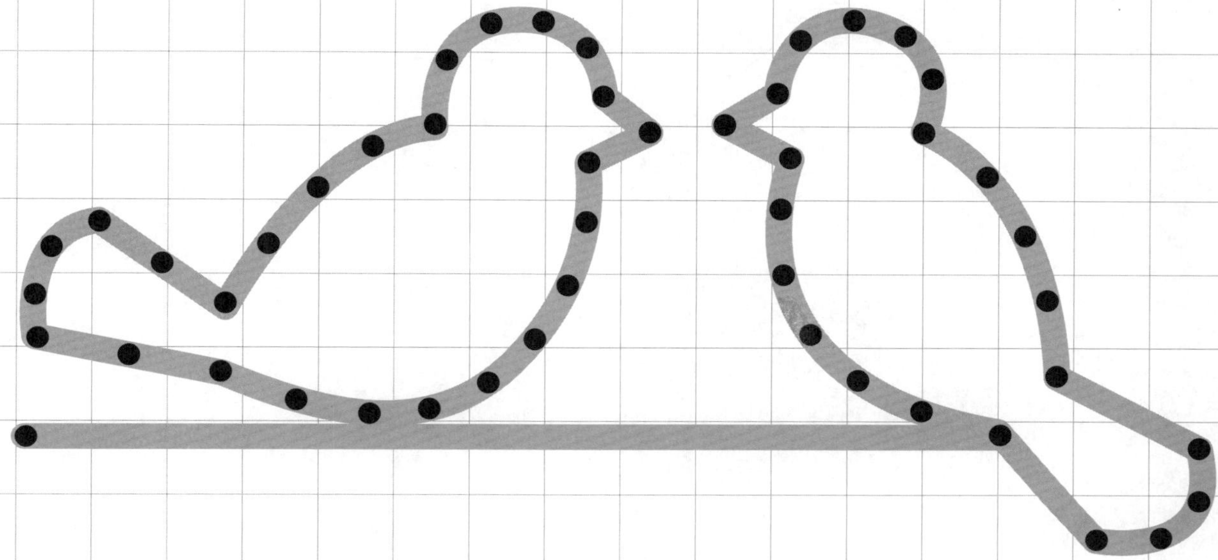

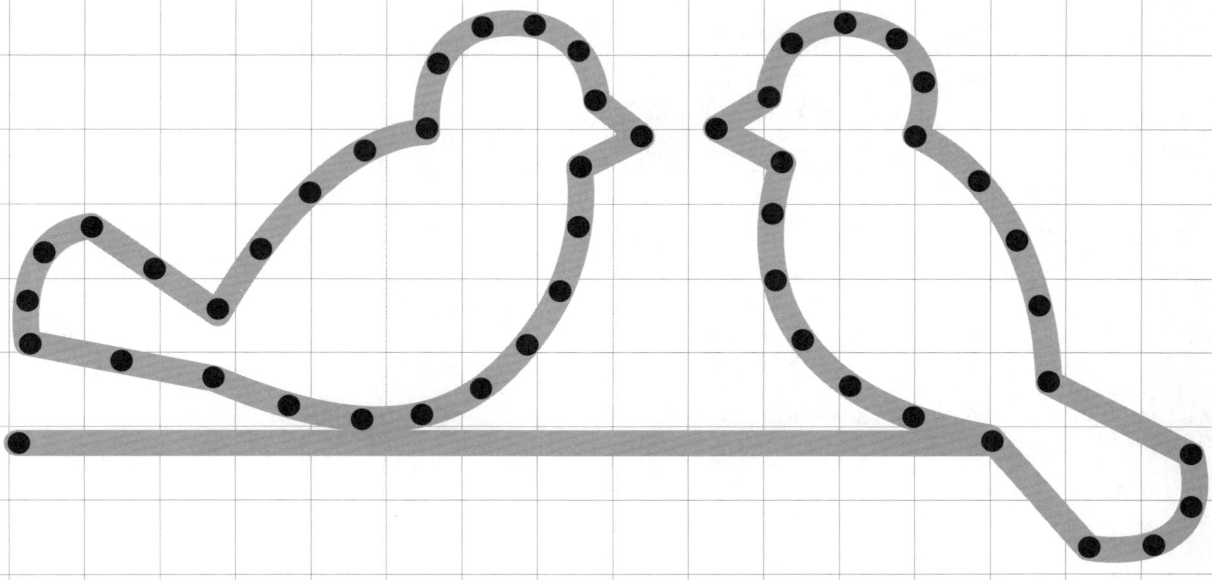

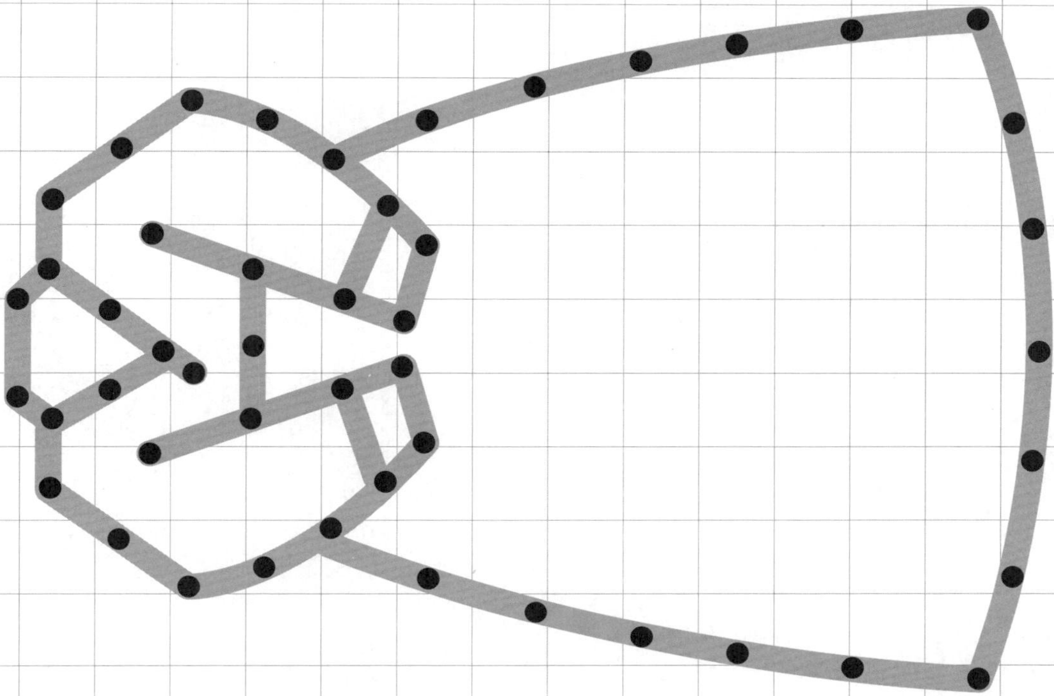

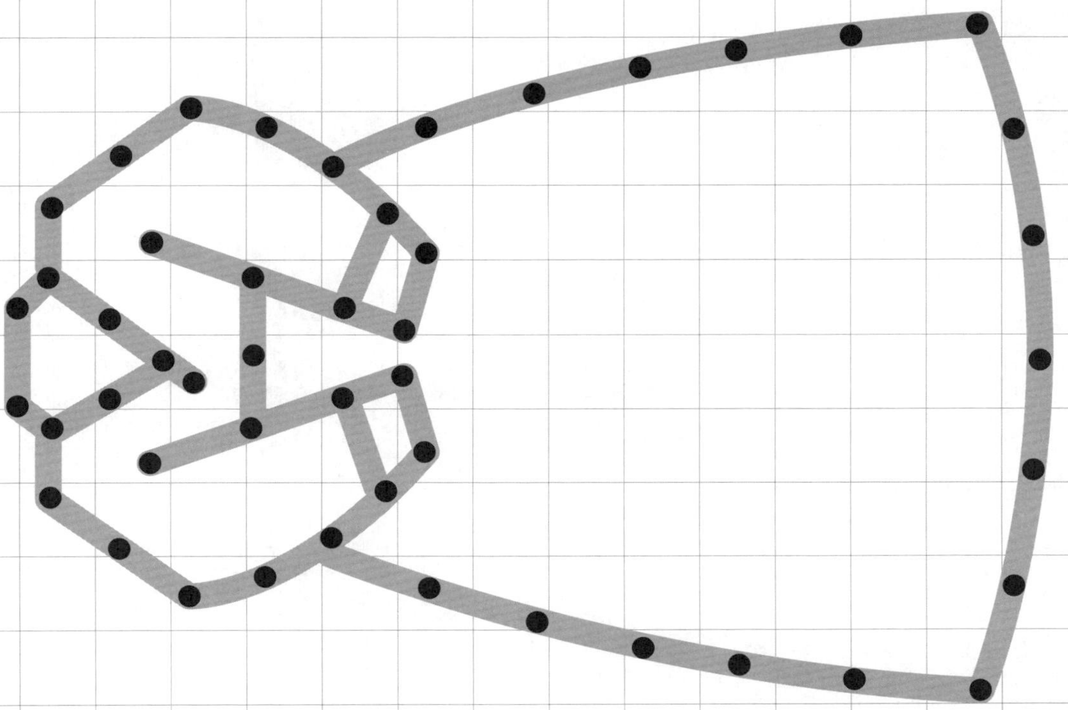

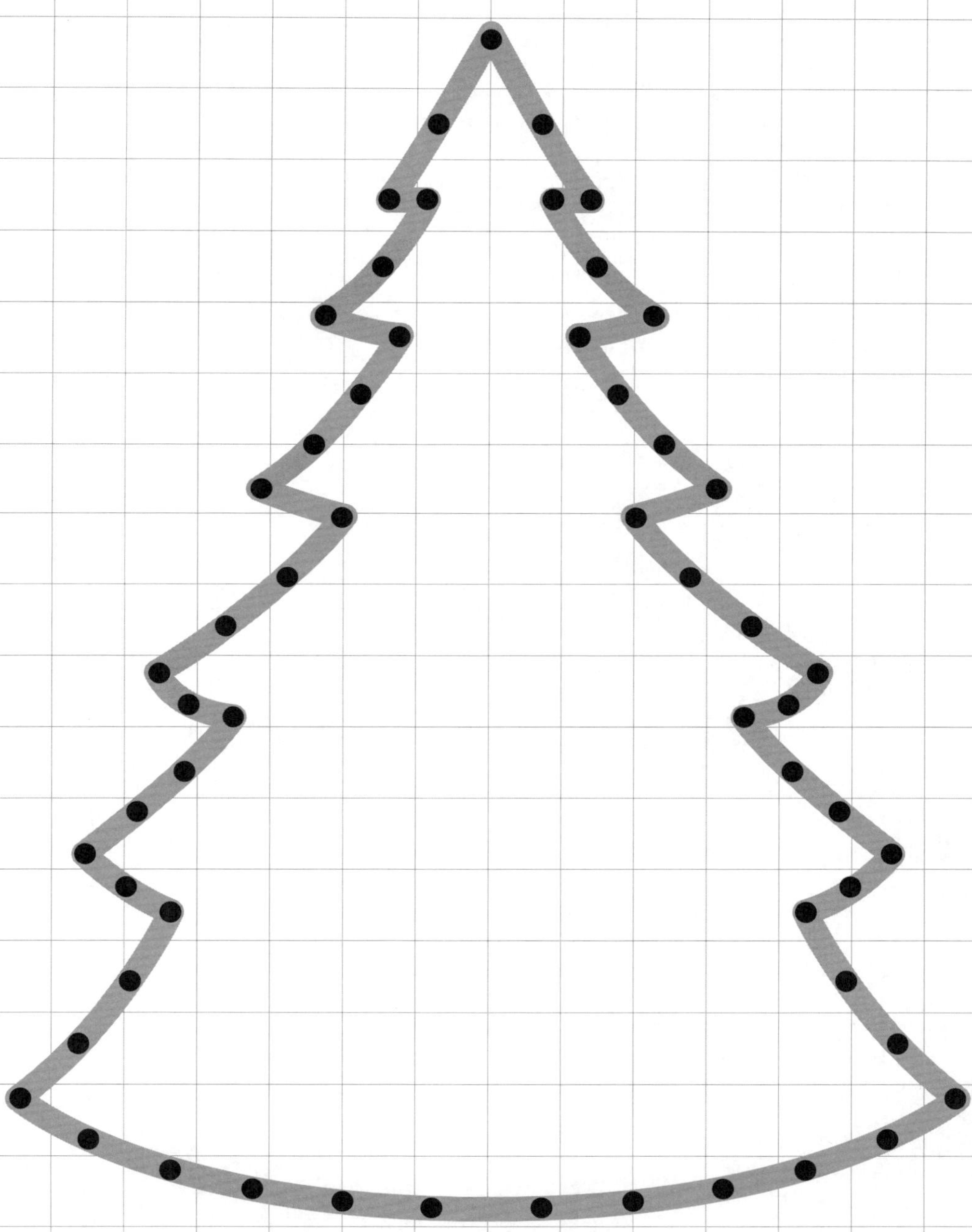

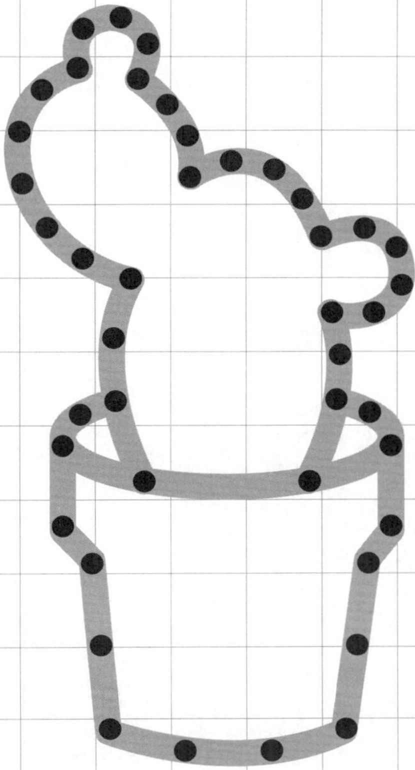
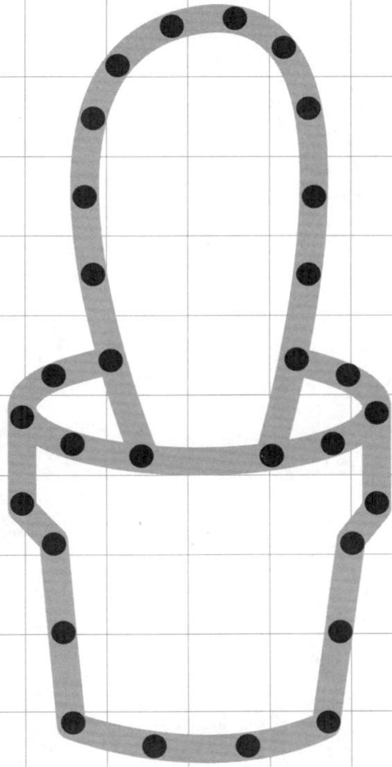
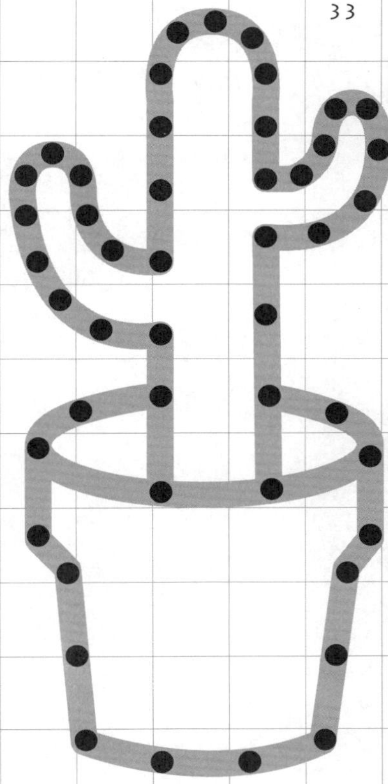
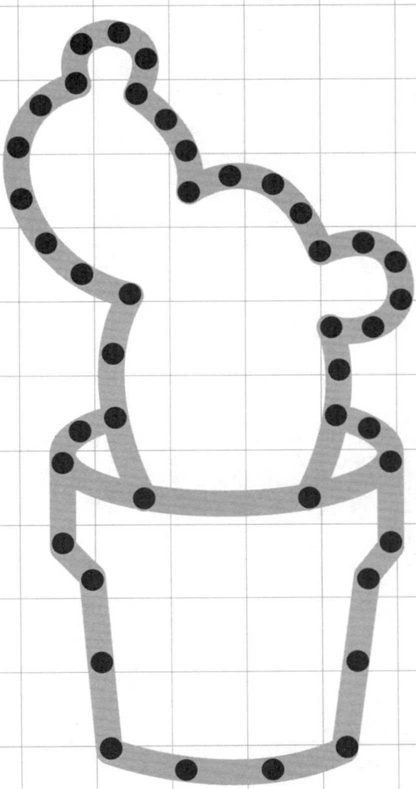
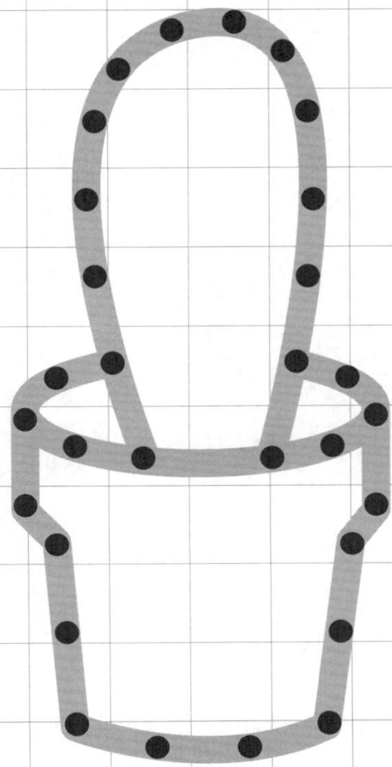
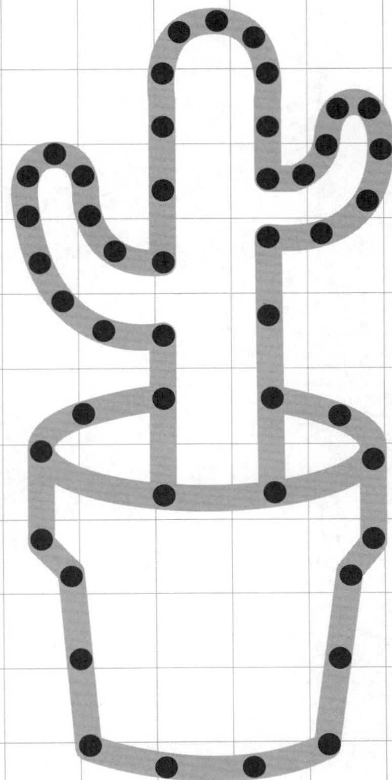

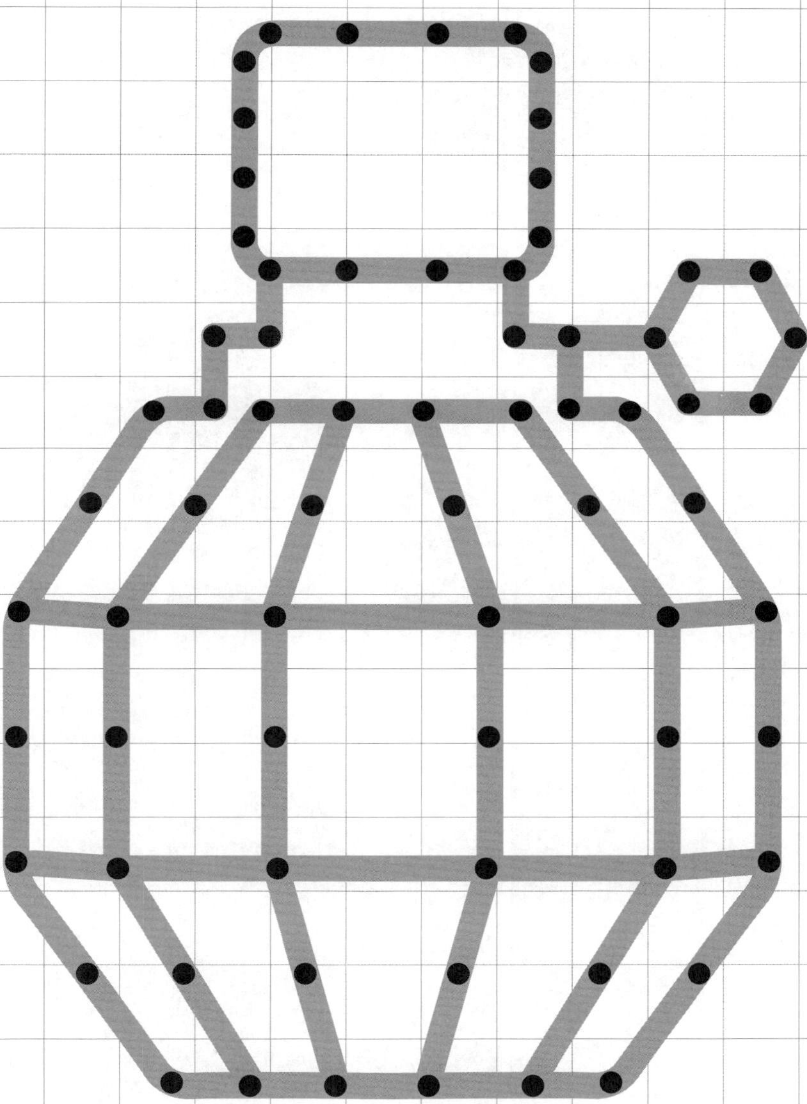

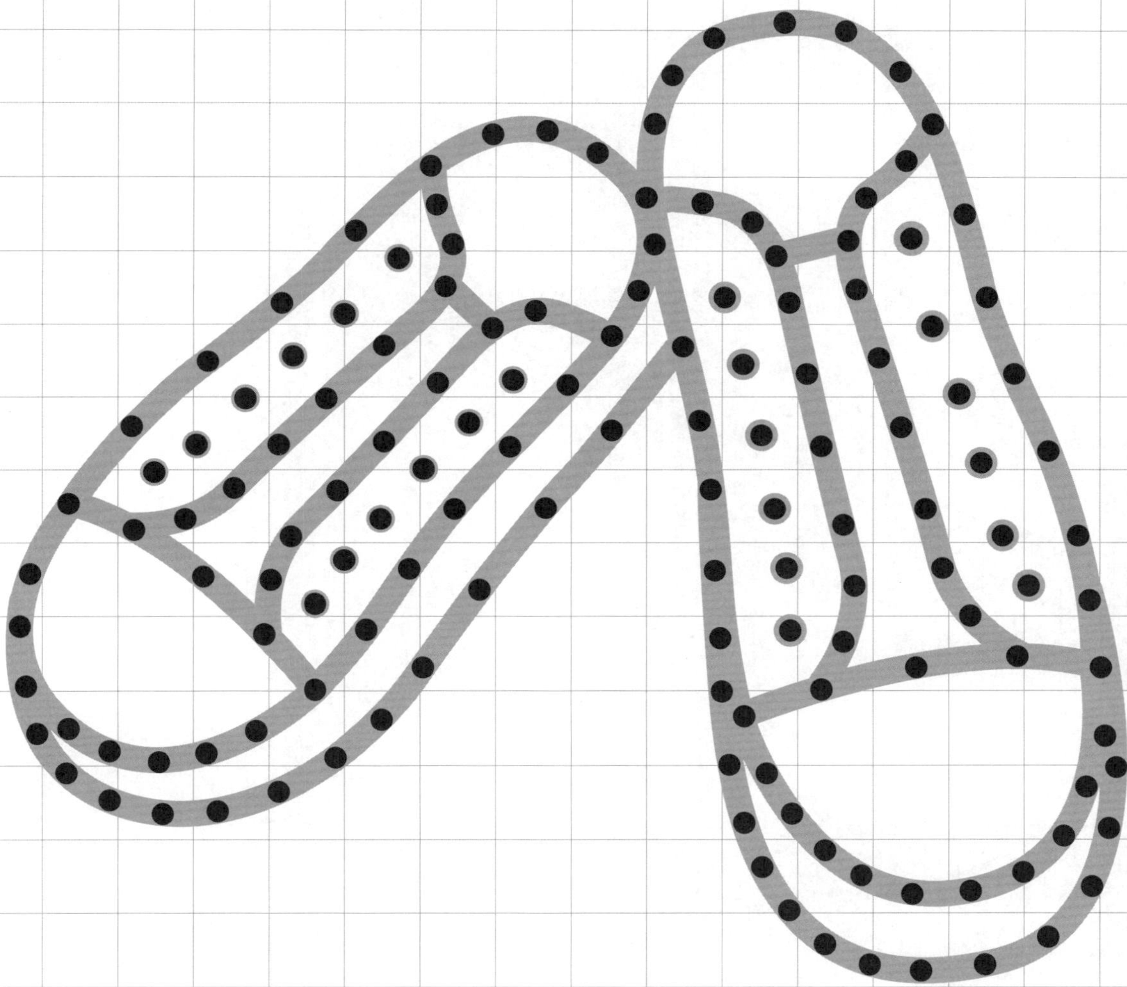

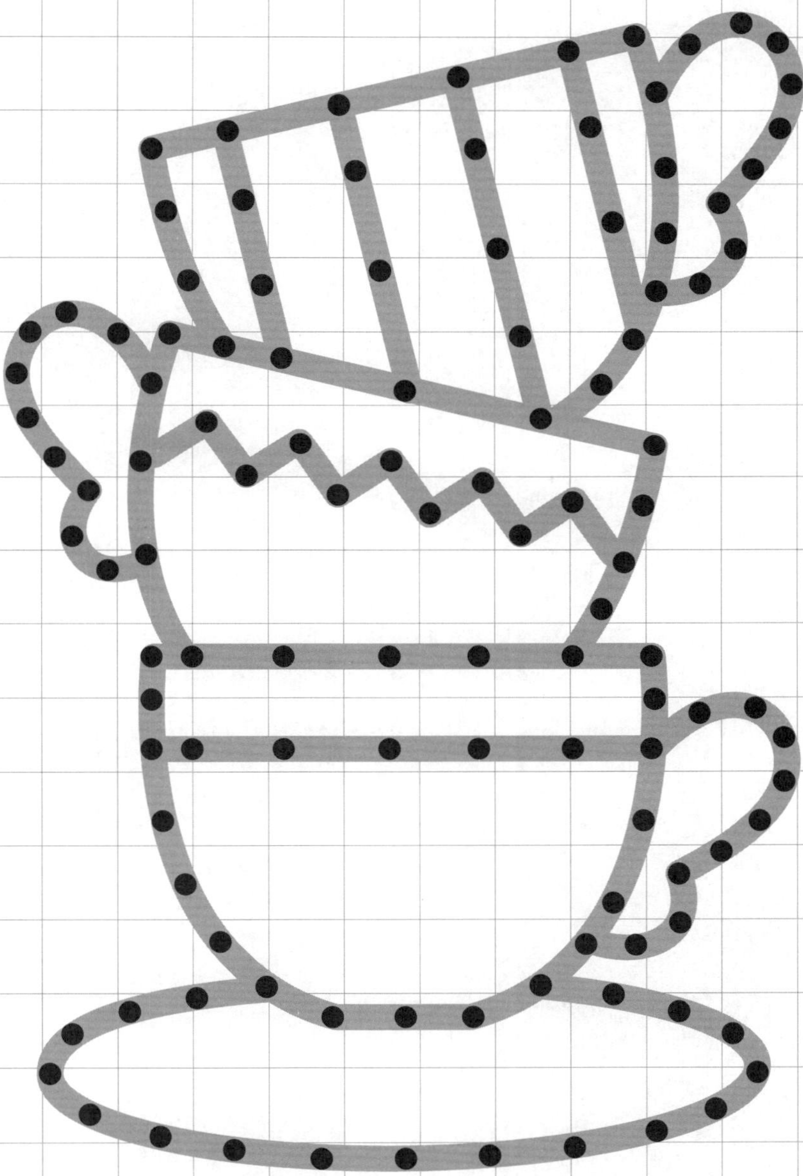

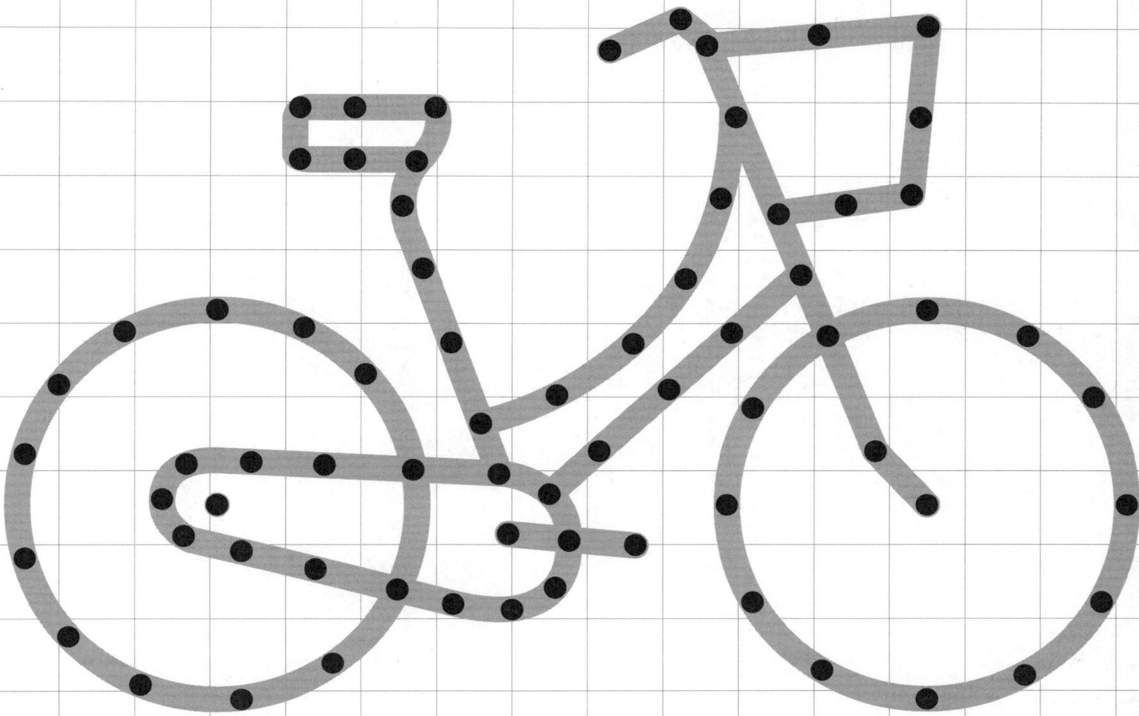

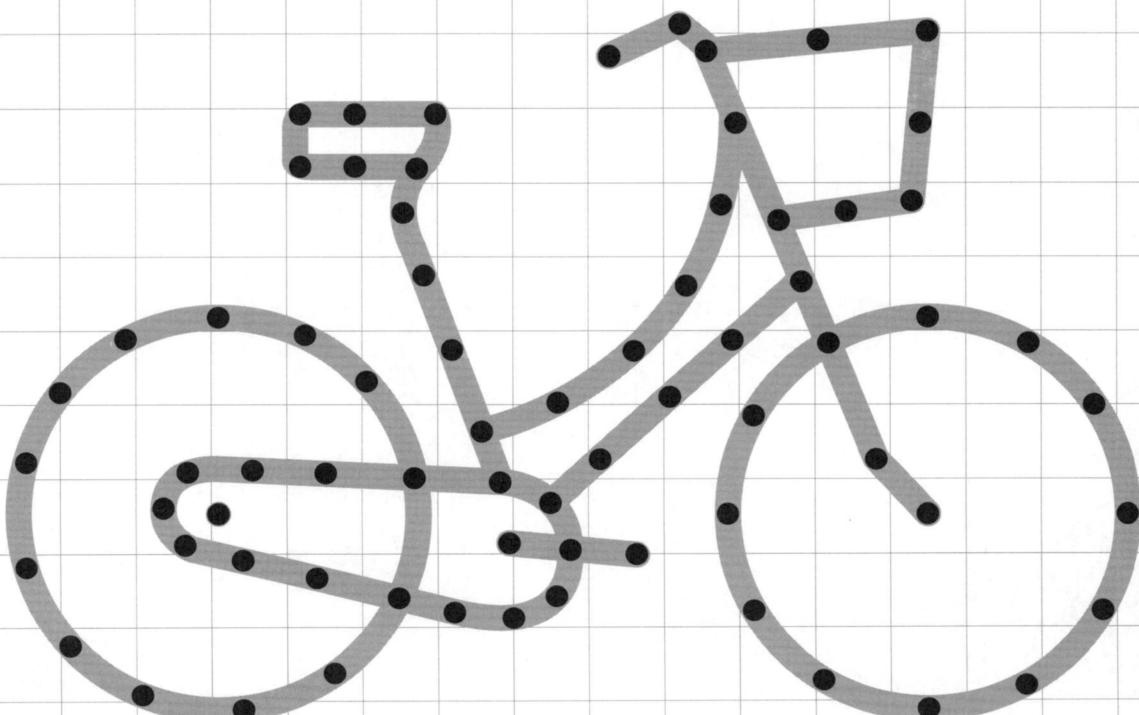

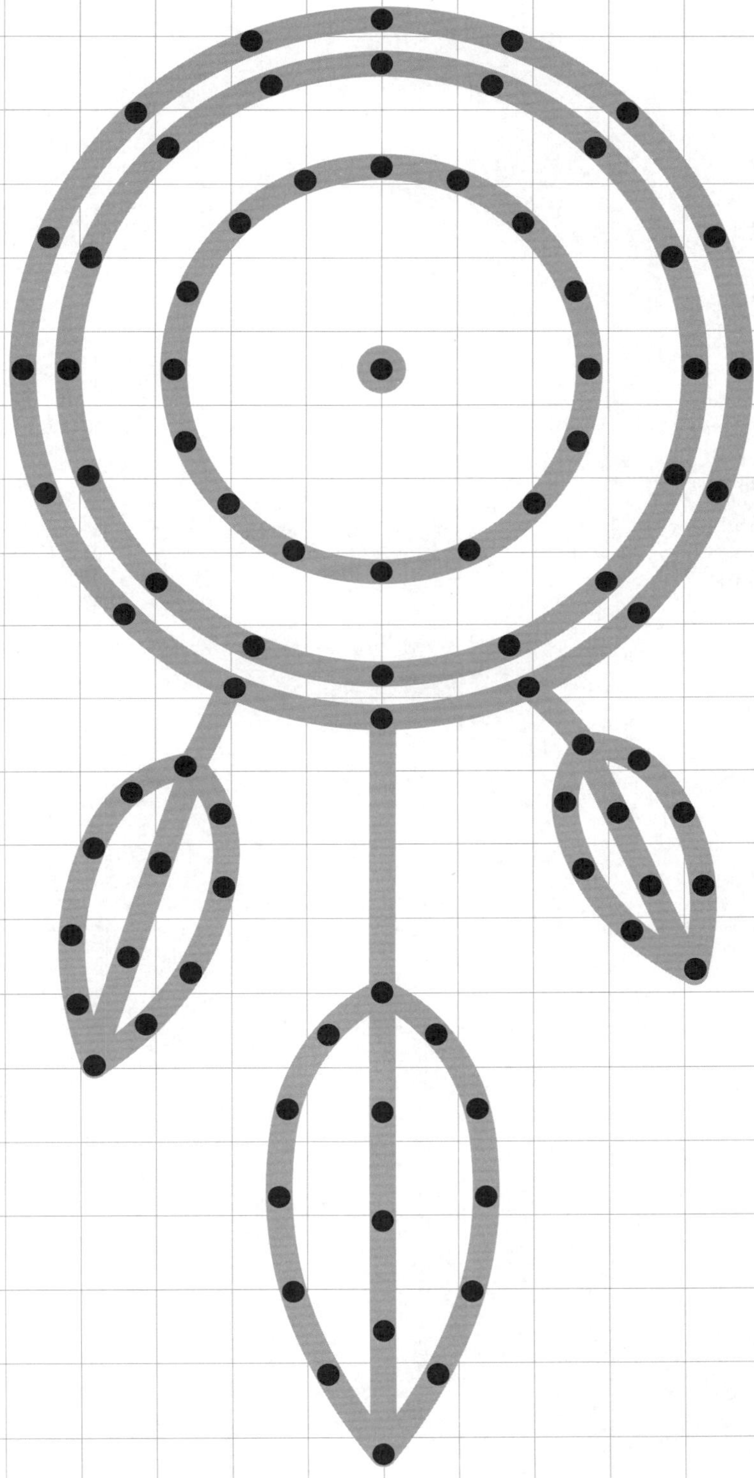

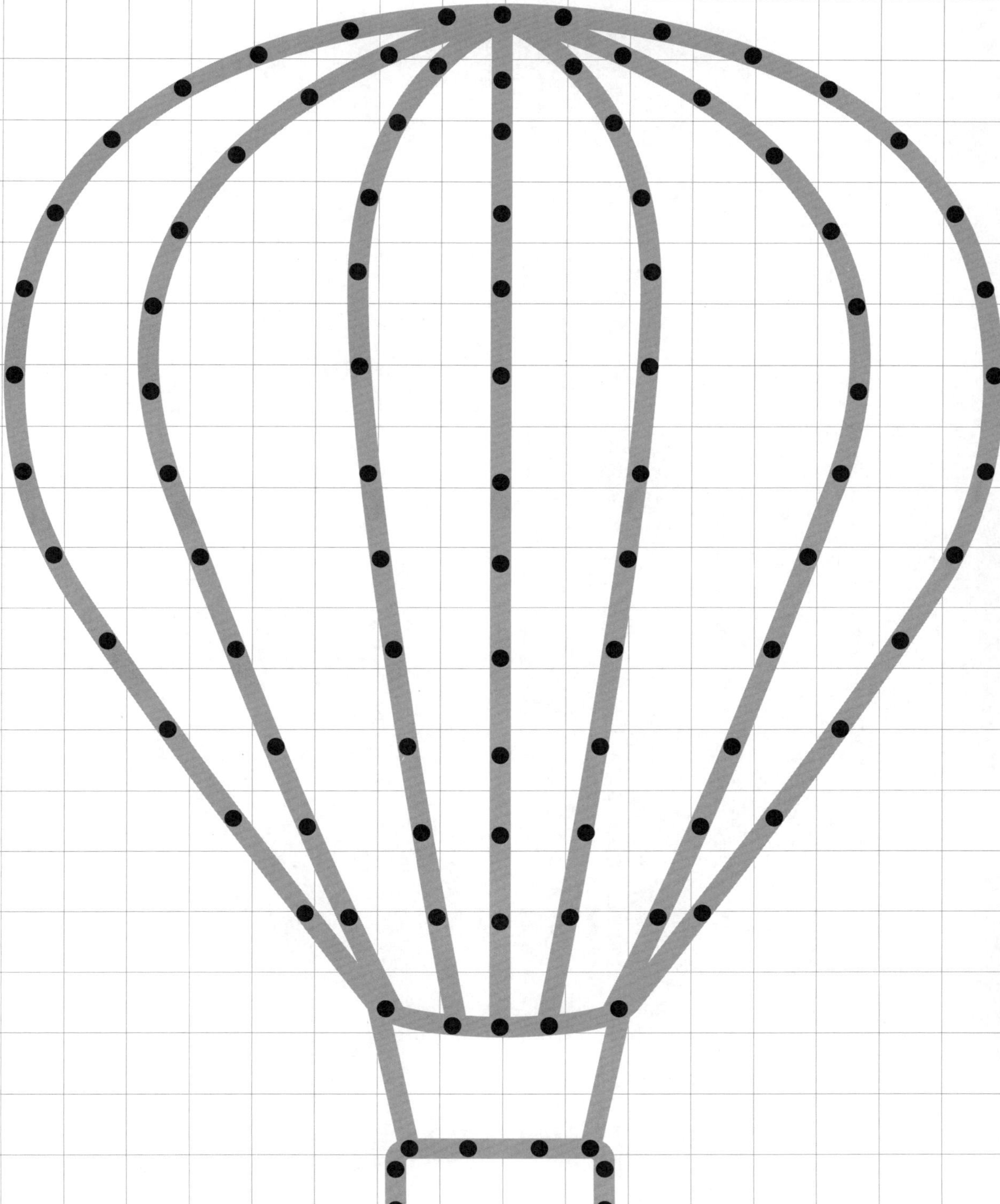

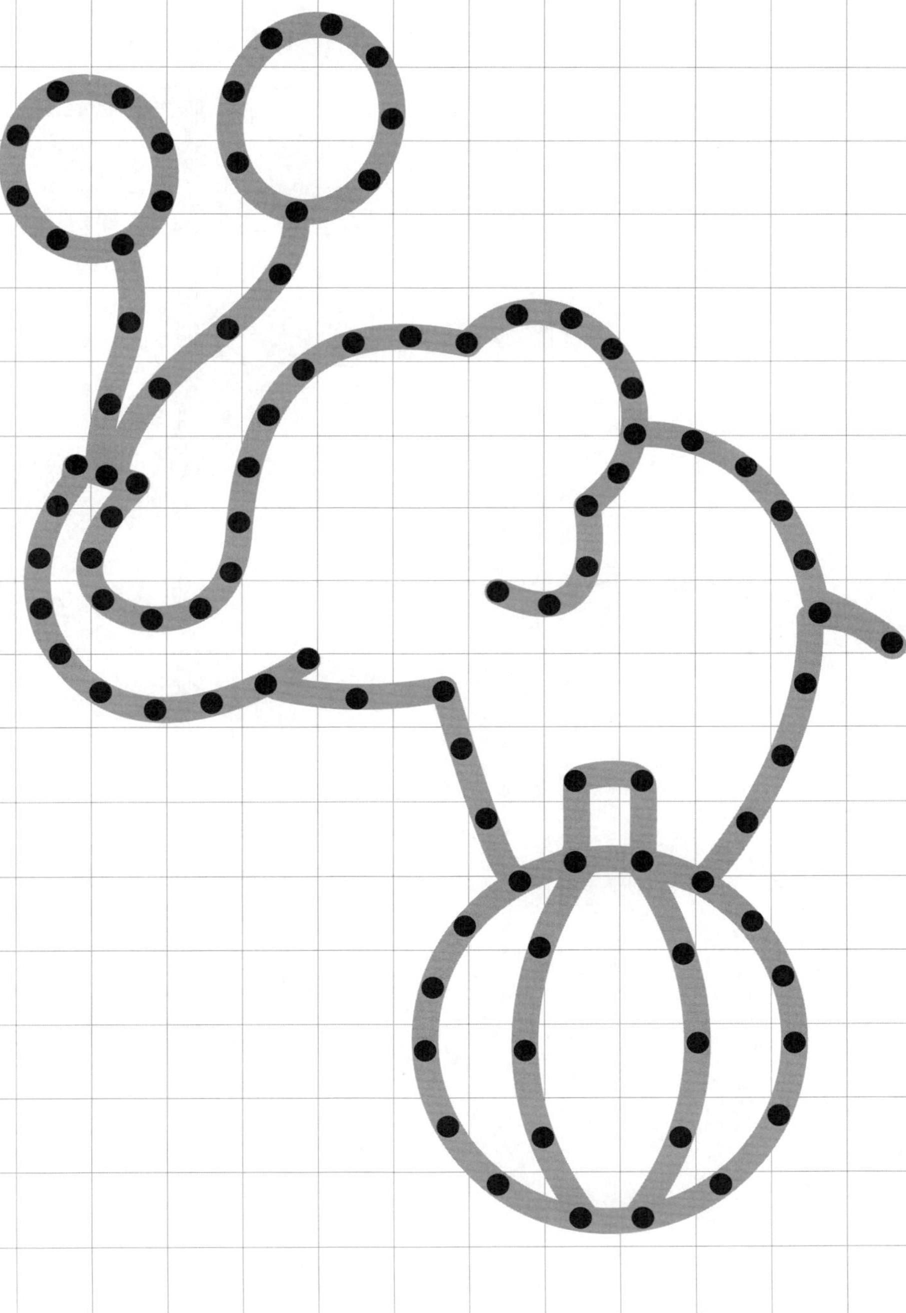

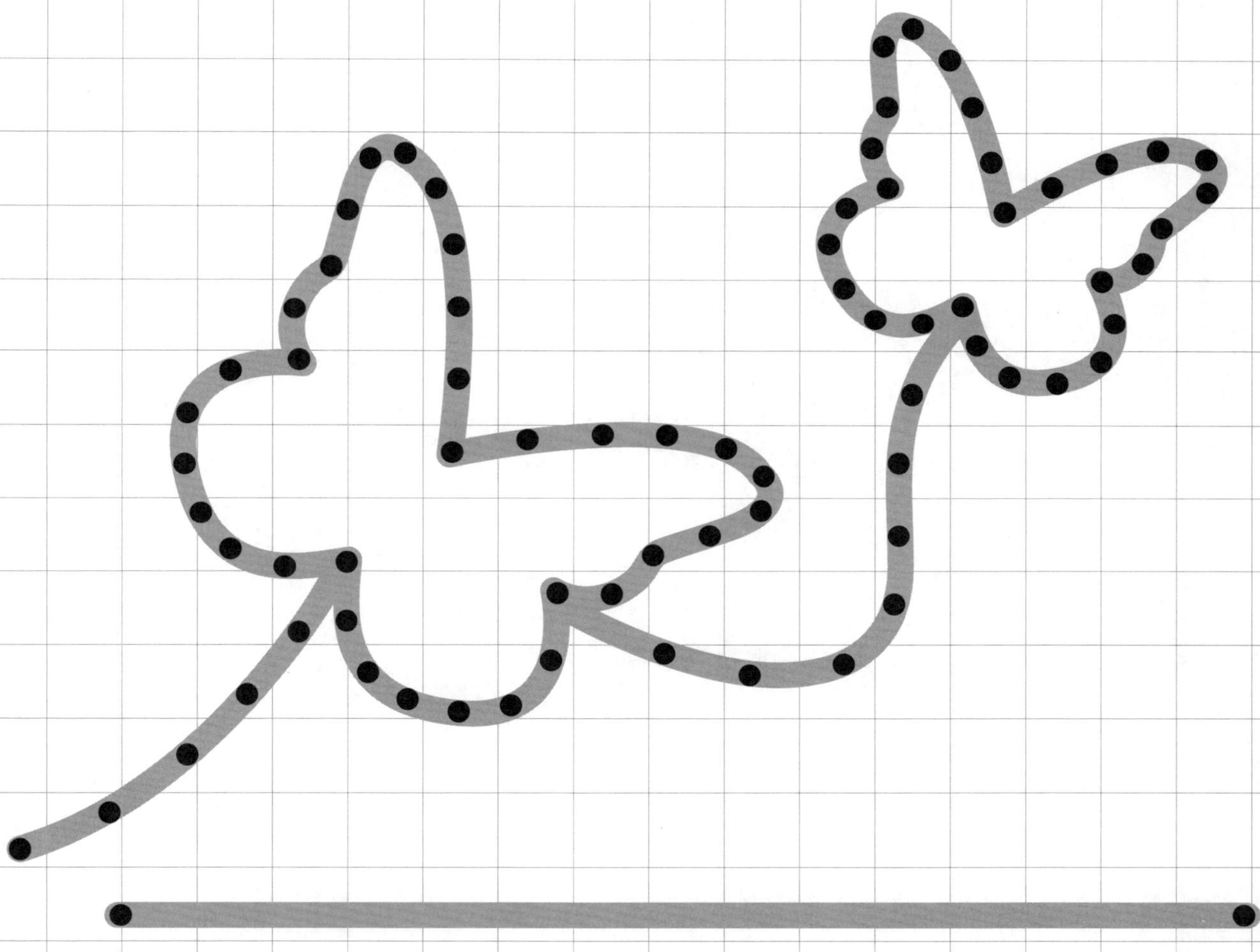

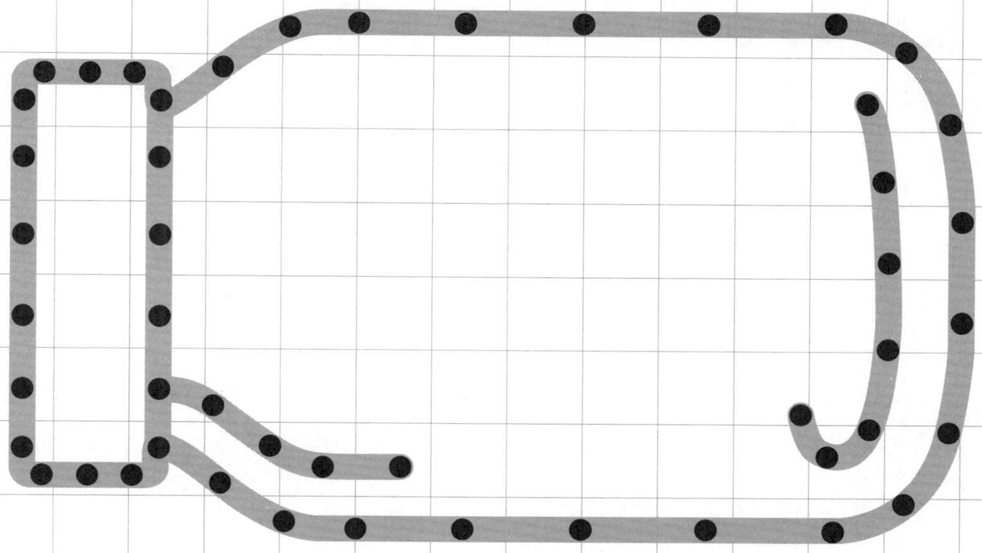

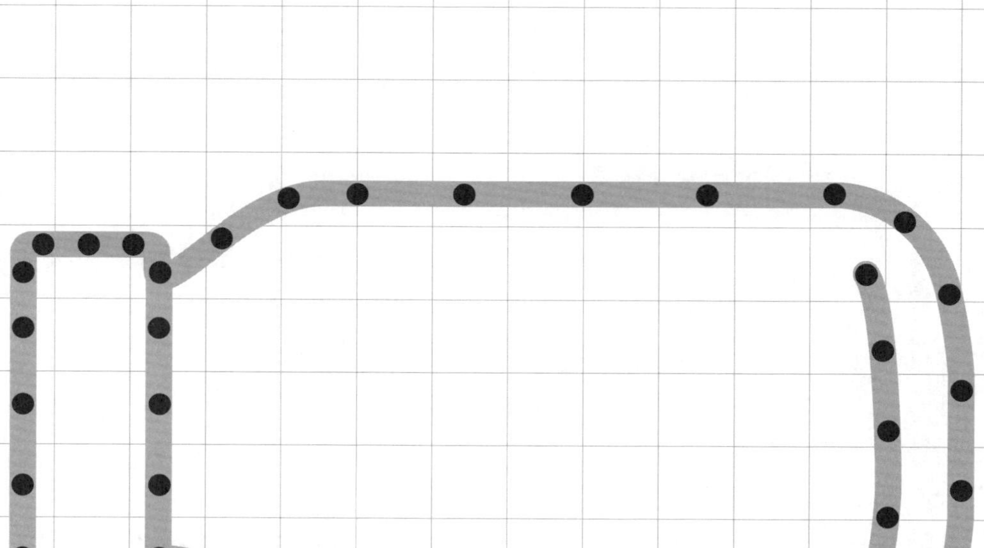

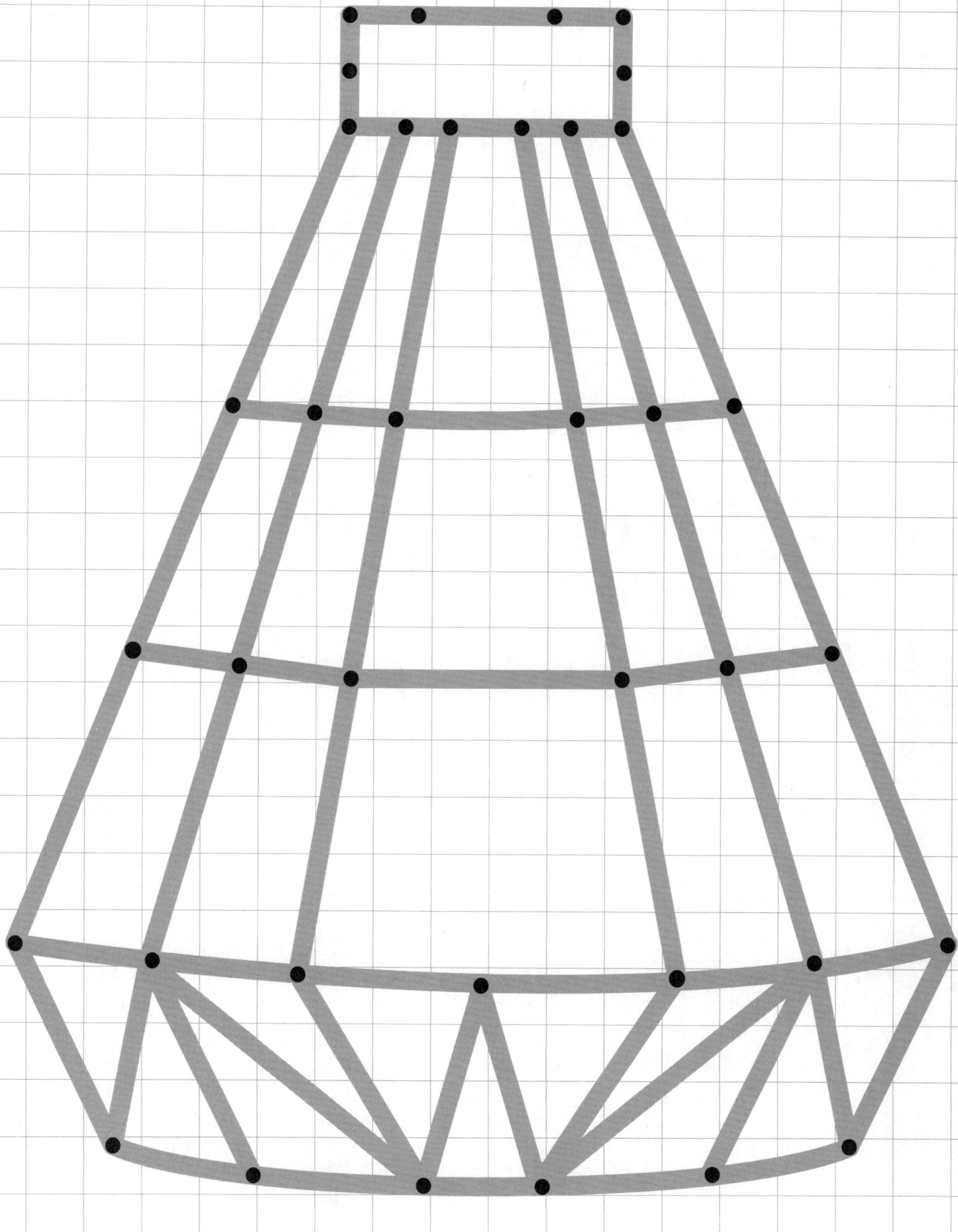

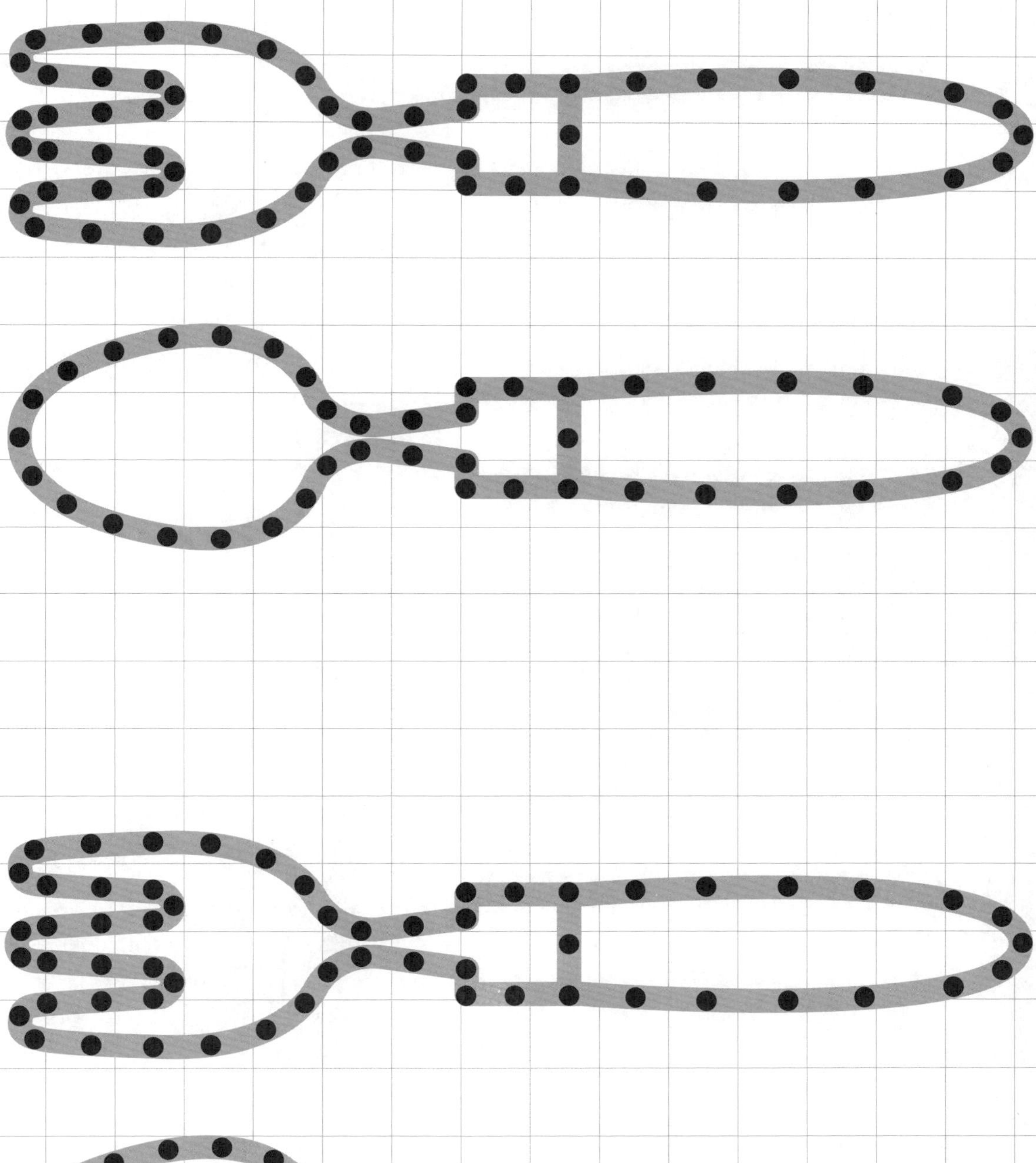

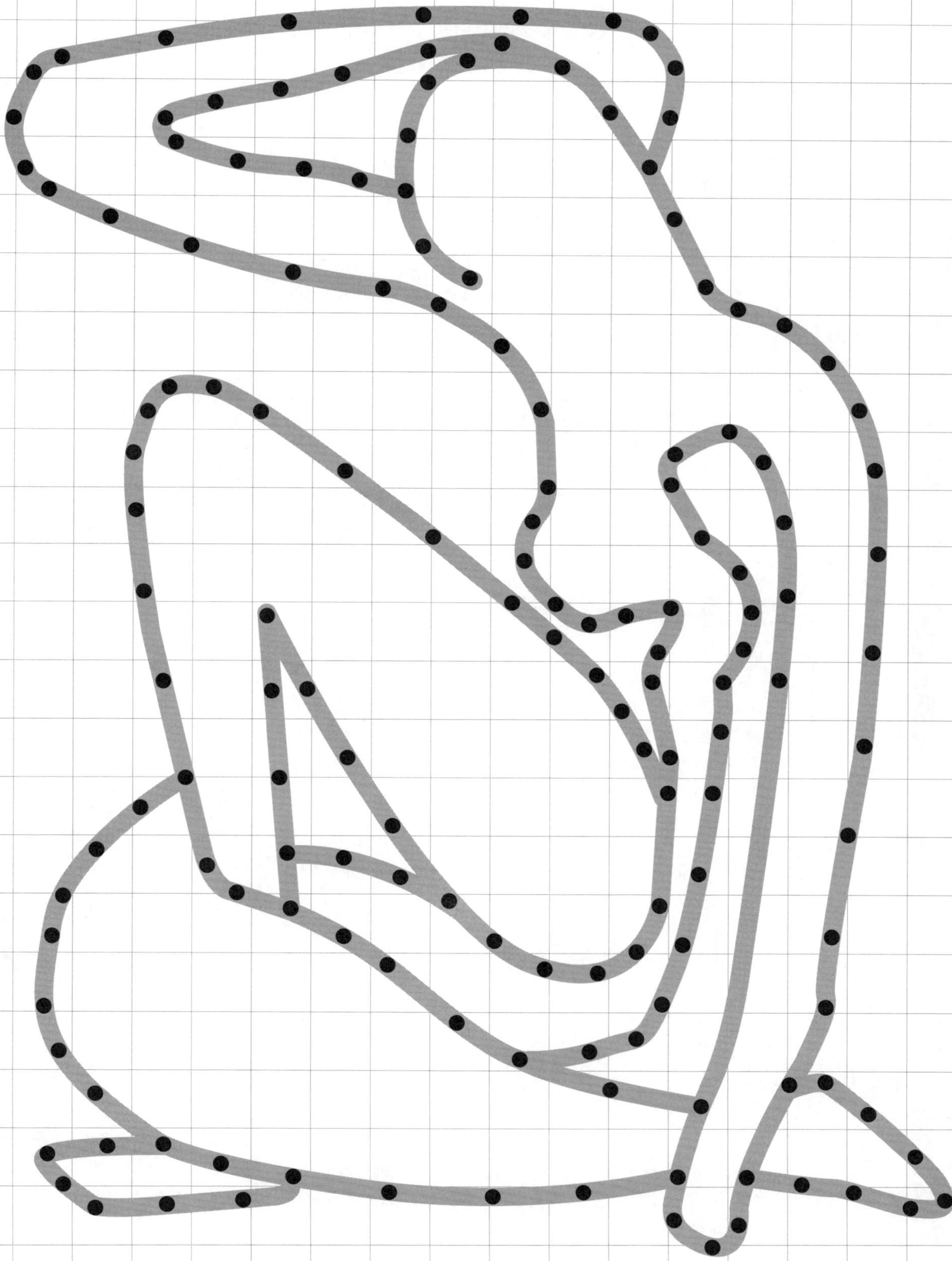